West Sweden
Including Gothenburg

the Bradt Travel Guide

James Proctor

edition
3

www.bradtguides.com

Bradt Travel Guides Ltd, UK

AUTHOR

James Proctor first travelled to West Sweden in 1986 and was smitten with Scandi-mania from the very outset – over the ensuing 30-plus years he's been back and forth ever since. Specialising in the Nordic countries, he has written a total of seven guidebooks, including one to the whole of Sweden as well as Bradt's *Faroe Islands* and *Lapland* guides. James speaks fluent Swedish, which Swedes (and most other people) find quite baffling. Searching to understand why, they regularly ask whether he has a Swedish mother or father. Their incredulity only grows when they learn that he learnt Swedish by mistake – beginning when he attended the wrong lecture at university!

Third edition January 2019
First edition published May 2014

Bradt Travel Guides Ltd
IDC House, The Vale, Chalfont St Peter, Bucks SL9 9RZ, England
www.bradtguides.com

Print edition published in the USA by The Globe Pequot Press Inc,
PO Box 480, Guilford, Connecticut 06437-0480

Text copyright © 2019 Bradt Travel Guides Ltd
Maps copyright © 2019 Bradt Travel Guides Ltd. Includes map data © OpenStreetMap contributors
Photographs copyright © 2019 Individual photographers (see below)
Project Manager: Susannah Lord

In collaboration with Västsvenska Turistrådet/West Sweden Tourist Board.

ISBN: 978 1 78477 638 1

British Library Cataloguing in Publication Data
A catalogue record for this book is available from the British Library

Photographs Goteborg & Co: Elisabeth Dunker, Emil Fagander, Dick Gillberg, Kjell Holmner, Stefan Karlberg/Liseberg, Per Pixel Petersson, Skyfliers, Beatrice Törnros, Jorma Valkonen; vastsverige.com: Mikael Almse, Göran Assner, Roger Borgelid, Åsa Dahlgren, Jonas Ingman, Gaby Karlsson Hain, Madeleine Landley, Jennie Lund, Monika Mano, Norrqvarn, Hans Schub, Henrik Trygg, Vitlycke Museum

Front cover Bohuslän coast village (Jonas Ingman)
Back cover Hiking in Dalsland (Roger Borgelid), Läckö Slott, Västergötland (Roger Borgelid)
Title page Kayaking near Fjällbacka (Henrik Trygg), *Kanelbullar* (cinnamon buns) (Jonas Ingman), Edshultshall (Jonas Ingman)

Maps David McCutcheon FBCart.S

Layout by Artinfusion
Production managed by Jellyfish Print Solutions; printed in the UK
Digital conversion by www.dataworks.co.in

Contents

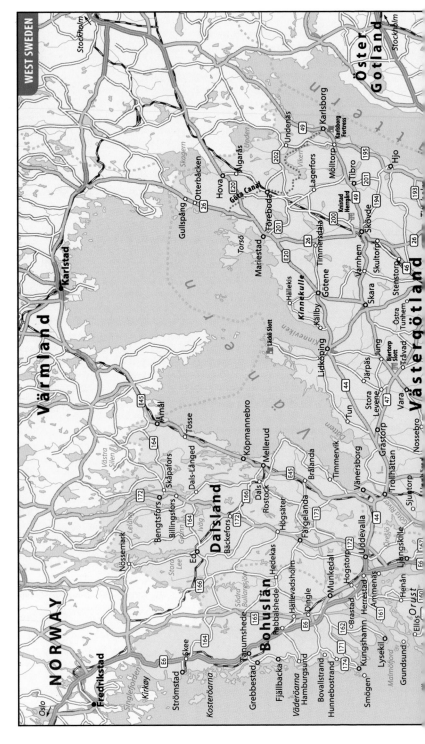

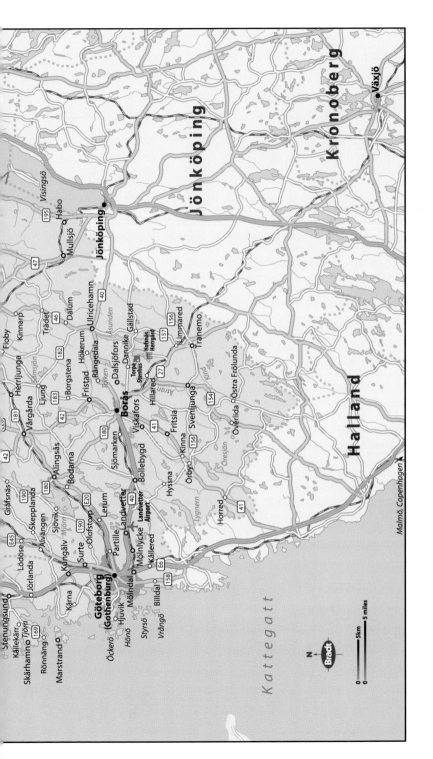

Introduction

Admittedly, the largest and best-known of all the Scandinavian countries, Sweden, for many people, is still a cold, remote and ruinously expensive place, lost somewhere on Europe's northern fringe. Sweden? Let alone West Sweden! Why would anyone want to go *there*?

First off, let's dispel a few misconceptions: with up to 20 hours of daylight in the summer, the average summer temperature in Gothenburg is much the same as in London; it's faster to fly from London to Gothenburg than it is to Barcelona; and lunch of succulent fresh fish served with locally sourced vegetables will cost considerably less than in London. With this guidebook in hand, the very first in English to the region of West Sweden, you will soon discover that this part of Sweden offers a tremendous variety of experiences to anyone looking for something a little different: hop on a boat and catch fresh mussels for lunch; paddle your own kayak round the archipelagos of the west coast; cycle through meadows of wild flowers along the banks of the Göta Canal … or simply find your own perfect *smultronställe* (the place where the wild strawberries grow), as the Swedes call it, perhaps by a lakeshore or a clearing in the forest, breathe the fresh air scented with pine and relish the unspoilt nature; this is what West Sweden is all about.

Gothenburg, the focal point of West Sweden, is a chic and cosmopolitan sort of place. Perfectly manageable in terms of size, this laid-back coastal city, criss-crossed by elegant boulevards and meandering canals, is a real treat. As you'd expect from art and style-conscious Sweden, the country's second city has a raft of excellent galleries and museums, which are sure to impress in their range as well as presentation. Gothenburg is also building a reputation for fine dining: a range of top-notch restaurants showcasing western Swedish cuisine take their cue from the sea; anything from juicy catfish or creamy lobster, soup, to fresh mussels with dill,

Skärhamn (Madeleine Landley)

or oysters served with slivers of tangy lime and ginger could be on the menu. What's more, Gothenburgers have an enviable reputation throughout the rest of Sweden for being friendly, down-to-earth and less reserved than their compatriots in other parts of the country. Together with their neighbours, they share a tremendous pride in their region and are genuinely delighted that more and more visitors are discovering this unique part of Sweden. Indeed, what helps to make West Sweden so very special is the glorious coastline which runs north from Gothenburg all the way to the Norwegian border. Spanning a distance of around 150km, the coast splinters into a bewildering array of 8,000 islands and skerries, whose sheltered waters are ideally suited to leisurely exploration by boat or kayak.

The **Bohuslän** coast is justifiably known for its angular granite rocks and outcrops, which have been worn silky smooth by the erosive action of the sea. The granite ranges in colour from earthy brown to dusky grey, though it is at its most alluring between the towns of Lysekil and Strömstad where it bears a pinky hue – at sunset the combination of the golden yellow of the sky, the aquamarine of the sea and the pink of the granite is a West Sweden classic.

Inland, Sweden's wooded heartland begins to show its face. Gone are the rocky outcrops of the western coastal shores and instead dense forests of spruce and birch dominate the landscape: this is **Dalsland** – a province that thrills in billing itself as Sweden in miniature. Notable towns and villages are few; instead this is a land of countless lakes (it has more lakes than any other region in Sweden), impressive rivers and the beginnings of the mountain chain that forms the border between Sweden and Norway, running all the way up to Lapland. Dalsland is a place to experience nature in the raw and, as such, offers a tantalising taste of the wilder side of Sweden, which proliferates in regions to the north of here.

East across Lake Vänern, **Västergötland** is predominantly a province of rich, flat agricultural land with a stirring Viking past, dotted with farm shops selling locally produced organic goods. However, in the east of the province, one of the region's defining features makes its mark: the 200km-long Göta Canal. Built in the early 1800s to connect Stockholm with Gothenburg, this masterpiece of engineering boasts no fewer than 58 locks, and enables boats to sail inland between the two cities in around four days. Today, three handsome, wooden passenger ships, the oldest dating from 1874 and designed to fit the narrowest of the locks like a glove, serenely ply the waters of the canal on their way between the Baltic and the North Sea.

This booklet contains only a selection of the spectacular places and sights on offer in West Sweden: use it as a starting point to head out and discover this beautiful region for yourself.

Dancing cranes at Hornborgasjön (Roger Borgelid)

WHEN TO VISIT

The summer months from June to August are always the best time to visit Sweden with long, sunny days and white nights, though be warned that July can be very busy with holidaying Swedes! However, spring and autumn, in particular May and September/October, can be delightful times to visit as West Sweden is much quieter at these times of year and, generally, the weather is still fine. Winter, though, is an altogether different matter: daylight is in short supply and there can be snow on the ground anytime from November to April; temperatures can fall to –10°C, although on the coast it's usually milder. Full climate and weather facts can be found at w smhi.se.

WILDLIFE

Sooner or later in West Sweden, you'll spot roe deer – they number around a million – and frequent fields and even private gardens. More elusive is the elk, which is also present in vast numbers – dawn and dusk are the best times for spotting them when they brave the open to feed. Note that there are no bears or reindeer in this part of Sweden. Of the region's birds, look out for cranes in early April which pair and dance at Hornborgasjön (page 73), while on the coast eider ducks, oystercatchers and Arctic tern are all common and easy to spot. In the forests of Dalsland, you may be lucky enough to see a Eurasian eagle owl – one of the biggest owls in the world.

PEOPLE, CULTURE AND ETIQUETTE

Swedes, in general, and the people of the west in particular, are polite and helpful. People in this part of the country tend to be more open and talkative than in other regions. Honesty is greatly cherished in Sweden and people mean what they say. Timekeeping is extremely important throughout the country as well – a meeting at 11.00 means just that – and arriving late is frowned upon and considered a sign of unreliability. On greeting people of either sex, you should shake hands while saying your name. If you're invited to someone's home for dinner, you should take a bottle of wine or some flowers.

WHERE IS WEST SWEDEN?

Occupying a V-shaped wedge of land, West Sweden is roughly the same size as the whole of Belgium. The region stretches from **Gothenburg** in the south to the Norwegian border in the north, from the **Skagerrak** strait in the west to the shores of one of Europe's three largest lakes and Sweden's biggest, **Vänern**, in the east.

In addition to Gothenburg (Göteborg in Swedish; pronounced *yur-tuh-BORI;* stress on last element), it comprises three provinces: coastal **Bohuslän**, which reaches from Gothenburg's northern border to Norway; undulating **Dalsland**, with its forests, lakes and rivers, west of Lake Vänern; and agricultural **Västergötland**, famous for the **Göta Canal**, which extends south and east of Vänern. Incidentally, Lake Vänern is four times the size of Greater London and even has its own shipping forecast.

HISTORICAL TIMELINE

800–500BC	Rock carvings made in present-day Bohuslän
1266	Statesman Birger Jarl dies in Västergötland
1298	Building begins on predecessor of Läckö Slott
1621	Gothenburg founded
1637	Expedition sails from Gothenburg to found New Sweden on Delaware River
1658	Sweden gains Bohuslän from Denmark and Norway
1731	Swedish East India Company founded
1775	Carlstens Fortress in Marstrand declared a free port
1810	Göta Canal begun
1822	Marstrand begins as bathing resort
1841	First shipyard founded in Gothenburg
1856	Train line reaches Gothenburg
1868	Dalsland Canal opens
1902	Trams begin running in Gothenburg
1915	Swedish–America line takes immigrants directly to the United States
1923	Liseberg amusement park opens
1927	Volvo produces first car in Gothenburg
1939	Götaälvsbron bridge opens
1962	Gothenburg-based Stena Line founded
1968	Tingstad tunnel under Göta River opens
1970	Skandiahamnen container begins operations
1994	Gothenburg opera inaugurated
	Rock carvings at Tanum included on the UNESCO World Heritage list
1998	Region of Västra Götaland (West Sweden) created
2006	Road tunnel under the Göta River opens in Gothenburg
2009	Inauguration of Sweden's only marine national park, Koster Sea
2011	Camilla Läckberg becomes Sweden's best-selling author
2021	Gothenburg will celebrate its 400th anniversary

COSTS AND TIPPING

Costs in West Sweden are generally in line with those you would expect to find in any other northern European country. Alcohol, when bought in a restaurant with a meal, can be pricey, less so if bought at the state alcohol store, Systembolaget, found in larger towns. Lunch is a particularly good bargain – a full set-meal at lunchtime, including salad and coffee, goes for around 85–100kr. A cup of coffee and a cinnamon roll in one of the region's many excellent cafés will cost around 65kr. It's common to round up a restaurant bill to the nearest sensible number rather than leaving a percentage tip. Taxi drivers don't expect a tip, whereas you mostly pay to check your coat in a restaurant or bar in winter – usually around 20kr. You can find up-to-date exchange rates at **w** xe.com.

GETTING THERE AND AWAY

BY PLANE Chances are you'll arrive in West Sweden by plane. Gothenburg's airport, **Landvetter** (GOT; **w** swedavia.se), is 25km east of the city and is linked to the city's main bus terminal, Nils Ericson Terminalen (adjacent to the train station), times and prices are available at **w** flygbussarna.se.

BY FERRY Gothenburg is linked to Germany and Denmark by regular ferries operated by **Stena Line** (**w** stenaline.se). Once daily, a ferry sails from the terminal at Jaegerdorffsplatsen to and from Kiel in northern Germany, whereas the more frequent ships to Fredrikshavn in Denmark use the terminal close to Masthuggstorget. Trams run between the city centre and both terminals.

DRIVING AND DISTANCES

West Sweden is larger than you might think when you first look at the map. Distances from north to south and east to west run to several hundred kilometres. As an idea of tried-and-tested distances and driving times, consider that the Göta Canal to coastal Lysekil is around 200km (3hrs by car); Gothenburg to Strömstad in northern Bohuslän is 165km (around 1hr 45mins); and Gothenburg to Åmål in Dalsland is 190km (2hrs 15mins). Although roads are generally good and well maintained, speed limits are strictly enforced with a burgeoning network of cameras; fines are brutal. A congestion charge applies when driving into Gothenburg – it is charged directly to your car hire company, who pass it on to you, whereas foreign-registered vehicles are exempt.

TOP ROAD TRIPS ACROSS WEST SWEDEN

Coastal scenery Take routes 160 and 161 from Stenungssund to Lysekil and cross the Gullmarsfjorden by free car ferry for a taste of the satisfyingly craggy coastline of Bohuslän.

Hilltop vistas Explore the enchanting country lanes of the Kinnekulle plateau for superb views out of Lake Vänern and the plains of Västergötland.

Backwoods West Sweden Drive the glorious switchback road Brudfjällsvägen, as it twists and turns and winds its way through deep forest between Håverud and Dals-Långed in Dalsland.

Hiking the lakes and hills of Dalsland is a popular activity (Roger Borgelid)

BY TRAIN There are direct trains (**w** sj.se) between Gothenburg and Copenhagen, where connections can be made to other destinations in Europe. There are also direct services to Oslo.

GETTING AROUND

The best way to explore West Sweden is by **car**. You'll find all the main car hire outlets in Gothenburg, with Hertz (**w** hertz.se) and Europcar (**w** europcar.se) located opposite the train station at Spannmålsgatan and in the main bus terminal, Nils Ericson Terminalen, respectively. Alternatively, a relatively comprehensive network of **trains** and **buses** covers the entire region, though getting to more off-the-beaten-track destinations requires perseverance. All **public transport** times are available at **w** resrobot.se or the official Västtrafik site (**w** vasttrafik.se). If you're planning on seeing the Gothenburg city region by public transport, consider the travel passes (see Västtrafik site for details) which allow unlimited travel for 24 hours (95kr) or 72 hours (190kr); buy them from any Västtrafik office, for example, at the Nils Ericson Terminalen. For more details on getting around Gothenburg, see box, page 18.

WHAT TO SEE AND DO

While in Gothenburg, be sure to visit one of Sweden's biggest and best art museums, the Konstmuseum, whose Fürstenberg galleries hold a superlative collection of early 20th-century Nordic art as well as contemporary art. Why not also take a canal tour aboard the open-topped Paddan boats which sail around the city and the harbour or try the Liseberg amusement park, Scandinavia's largest? In the Gothenburg archipelago, hiring a bike is the thing to do, exploring the islands at

---

WEST SWEDEN'S TOP THINGS TO DO

Canal tour Take a slow boat ride on either the Dalsland or the Göta Canal (see boxes, pages 62 and 63).

Coffee and cake The Swedes call it *fika* and you can't get more Swedish than a good cup of coffee with a cinnamon bun or a piece of cake.

Farm shops Sample and buy tasty, homemade produce from the region's farmers (see box, page 73).

Hiking Commune with nature: roam along the Pilgrim's Trail (see box, page 58), explore car-free islands, and trek the wild forests of Dalsland.

Island hopping Take a ferry out to the islands off Sweden's west coast (see box, page 39), and why not go hiking or biking?

Liseberg Ride the rollercoasters at Gothenburg's fabulous amusement park (see box, page 25).

Prehistoric art Marvel at 3,000-year-old Bronze Age rock carvings at Vitlycke (page 50).

Road trip Fall in love with the switchback road between Håverud and Dals-Långed (see box, page 11).

Sea kayaking Explore the Bohuslän coast from a kayak (see box, page 41).

Seafood Treat yourself to some of the freshest you've ever tasted (see box, page 44).

Wild swimming Plunge into crystal-clear water surrounded by towering pine forest (see box opposite).

your own pace – ideally with a picnic. On the Bohuslän coast, you're spoilt for choice: sea kayaking or perhaps a seafood safari; take a boat out to some of the coast's enchanting islands; check out ornate rock carvings from the Bronze Age or visit the Nordic Watercolour Museum. Alternatively, come face to face with some of the world's most endangered species at Nordens Ark or walk in the footsteps of the characters from the novels of Camilla Läckberg – Sweden's best-selling author. In Dalsland, try a spot of canoeing or horseriding through some spectacular scenery or jump on two wheels and cycle part of the Göta Canal in Västergötland. Though don't forget the fairy-tale castle, Läckö Slott, or the breathtaking Neolithic burial site, Ekornavallen, with its impressive graves and standing stones.

Winter kayaking in Bohuslän (Roger Borgelid)

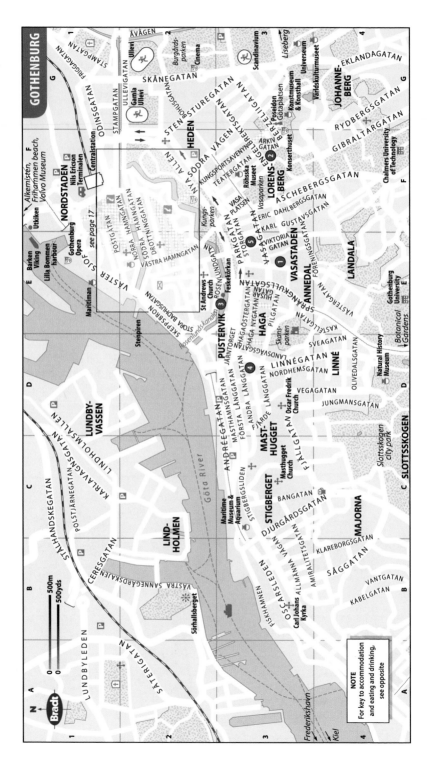

GOTHENBURG

1

Gothenburg

Dominating the entire west coast of Sweden, handsome Gothenburg (Göteborg) is an instantly likeable place. The city, Sweden's second largest with a population today of around half a million, was actually designed by the Dutch, world experts in the early 1600s in draining and building on marshland. By order of the Swedish king, the Dutch dug a total of four canals to channel water into the Göta River – two of them remain. Indeed, Gothenburg's layout of streets and canals bears a striking resemblance to that of the Indonesian capital, Jakarta, which was also built by the Dutch at the same time. Founded in 1621 and occupying a prime location on the shores of the Kattegatt (an arm of the North Sea), at the mouth of the Göta River, Gothenburg has traditionally sought its fortunes through sea-borne trade. The Swedish East India Company, established a century or so later in 1731, generated considerable wealth through commercial links, particularly with China. Many of the city's imposing classical stone buildings, often lining the canals, were built around this time; one fine example is Ostindiska Huset, which once served as the company's headquarters. Over the centuries, a succession of Dutch, German and Scottish merchants settled in Gothenburg – sometimes founding commercial dynasties, sometimes simply securing a proportion of the city's lucrative trade for themselves. Gothenburg has always been an international city, and that cosmopolitan spirit lives on today.

Although herring fishing was a big money-spinner for the city during the 19th century, by the 1850s Gothenburg's sizeable harbour had instead become the natural departure point for the 1.3 million Swedes who emigrated to the United States in search of a better life. Initially ships sailed to Hull in England, from where passengers travelled by train to Liverpool for the final leg of the journey, though from 1915 ships sailed directly from Gothenburg to America. During the 19th and 20th centuries, manufacturing was an integral part of the city's economy – not only is Gothenburg the home of Volvo (founded in 1926), but it's also the base for the SKF ball-bearing factory and one of the main sites for telecommunications giant Ericsson. Shipbuilding may well be less important today than during the 1970s and 1980s, but Gothenburg remains the largest port in Scandinavia and headquarters to Europe's biggest ferry company, Stena Line.

ORIENTATION

Central Gothenburg can be divided into three main areas: the grid of streets between the Göta River and Centralstation [14 F1], which lie north of the Stora Hamnkanalen canal; the shopping streets south of the canal, located between the Trädgårdsföreningen park [17 D2] and the river; Kungsportsavenyn – known locally as simply Avenyn – and the area south of Kungsportsplatsen square [17 C2], dominated by Kungsportsavenyn – known locally as simply Avenyn – the city's main boulevard. Out of the centre, there are again three main areas worthy of exploration: studenty Vasastaden [14 E3], west of Avenyn, with its fine 19th-century and National Romantic architecture; the former working-class district of Haga [14 E3], west of Vasastaden, now a haven of trendy cafés and restaurants; and, finally, Linné [14 D4], west and south of Haga, which includes the glorious Slottsskogen park and botanical gardens.

DROTTNINGTORGET AND AROUND

No matter whether you arrive in Gothenburg by train or airport bus, you'll be deposited at the combined (and impressively efficient) bus and train station which features the Centralstation [14 F1] (for trains) and the adjoining Nils Ericson Terminalen [14 F1] (for buses). You can walk undercover between the two sections. Although extensively rebuilt, the train station is the oldest in Sweden still in operation, dating from 1858, and, immediately outside the station in Drottningtorget square, you'll find the city's original railway hotel, now Hôtel Eggers. Not only is this cavernous place reputed to be haunted, it also has had

Central Gothenburg on the banks of the Göta River (Skyfliers)

GOTHENBURG
City Centre

For listings, see page 19

Where to stay	
1	Avalon.....................................C2
2	Clarion Post...........................D1
3	Comfort Hotel Göteborg.....A1
4	Hotel Royal............................D1
5	Hotel Vanilla..........................B2

Where to eat and drink	
6	Bar Centro.............C2
7	Bhoga...................B1
8	Da Matteo..............B3
9	Rosenkaféet.........D1

quite an eventful past: many an emigrant slept here before boarding a ship to the New World; refugees from the Russian Revolution were taken in here; and secret negotiations between the Allies and the Nazis on the exchange of prisoners took place here during World War II.

In addition to the criss-cross of tram lines in the square (this is one of Gothenburg's main tram interchanges), the square is best known for the hulking Neoclassical building on its eastern flank: the former central post office (*posthuset*) and now the inordinately stylish Clarion Post hotel [17 D1]. Designed and completed in 1925 and built of Bohuslän granite, the building is now listed: neither the ornate façade, with its intricate carvings and pillars, nor features, such as the original former cash hall inside, may be altered.

WEST TO THE GÖTA RIVER

From Drottningtorget, Norra Hamngatan heads west along Stora Hamnkanalen to the Göta River. Stretching north from the canal all the way up to Kanaltorgsgatan, **Nordstan** [17 C1] is one place that's hard to miss. As it's one of Sweden's largest indoor shopping centres, you're bound to end up here sooner or later. Today's shopping emporium is built over an area cleared of sprawling slums – in fact, the former streets still run their old course through the shopping centre, bearing their original names: Postgatan, for example, which passes right through the middle of Nordstan from west to east, was once the heart of Gothenburg's red light district and a den of iniquity. Inside, you'll find some of Sweden's best-known chain stores such as the Åhléns department store, the DIY-lover's dream that is Clas Ohlson and the Akademibokhandeln bookstore.

The most cost-effective way to get around Gothenburg – and to see some of the sights and attractions – is to get a **Göteborg Pass** from one of the tourist offices or online at **w** goteborg.com. Prices vary from 345kr for one day (24hrs) to 995kr (5 days) and include free entry to museums, a boat tour of the archipelago, a city bus tour and the Liseberg amusement park, as well as a host of other benefits. Full details are online. Alternatively, **travelpasses** for 24 hours (95kr) or 72 hours (190kr), allowing unlimited rides on buses, ferries and trams, are available from travel information offices or newsagents. You cannot buy tickets on board buses or trams with cash. For more information, see **w** vasttrafik.se.

GUSTAV ADOLFS TORG [17 B1] Exiting Nordstan from its western edge or simply continuing along Stora Hamngatan from Drottningtorget, you'll soon reach Gustav Adolfs Torg. In the middle of this cobbled square, atop a stone plinth, proudly stands a copper **statue** of Gothenburg's founding father, **King Gustav II Adolf**, gesticulating to the spot he declared his city should be built. The square is flanked to the west by the neoclassical **Rådhuset** (town hall; 1672) designed, like so many other of Sweden's grand buildings, by Nicodemus Tessin the Elder, and to the north by **Stadshuset** (city hall; 1746) and **Börsen** (stock exchange; 1849).

STADSMUSEUM [17 B1] (Norra Hamngatan 12; **w** stadsmuseum.goteborg.se; admission 60kr) A block or so further west stands one of Gothenburg's most

imposing brick buildings: the **Ostindiska Huset**. Built between 1750 and 1762, it once housed the offices, auction house and storerooms of the Swedish East India Company and is today home to the city's biggest museum, the Stadsmuseum. Established in 1731 to conduct trade with the Far East (and to compete with similar trading companies in Holland and Britain), the Swedish East India Company held the sole rights to trade with China and became the largest company in Sweden during the 18th century until it ceased operations 80 years later. All imported goods such as tea, silk and porcelain were sold at auction in Gothenburg and the Swedish state received a proportion of all sales in taxes. A reminder of the Chinese influence which pervaded Gothenburg society at this time can be found on the second floor of the museum where there are also several collections of delicate porcelain.

A replica of the East Indiaman *in Gothenburg harbour (Elisabeth Dunker)*

However, it's the museum's exhibition of **Viking** artefacts that is considerably more engaging. The prize exhibit is the Äskekärr longboat, a trading vessel from around AD900 which was found along the Göta River and which, uniquely, bears a runic inscription thought to refer to the livestock it once carried. Elsewhere, don't miss the medieval church art, especially the 2m-tall wooden carving of the Archangel Michael, dating from the mid-1200s, and the magnificent triptych of Nordic saints from the church of Kulling-Skövde in Västergötland.

TOP 5 PLACES TO STAY, EAT AND DRINK IN GOTHENBURG

TOP 5 PLACES TO STAY

🏠 **Avalon** [17 C2] Kungstorget 9; 031 751 02 00; e info@avalonhotel.se; w avalonhotel.se; dbl from 1,270kr. Design hotel.

🏠 **Comfort Hotel Göteborg** [17 A1] Skeppsbroplatsen 1; 031 752 28 00; e co.goteborg@choice.se; w nordicchoicehotels.se/hotell/sverige/goteborg; from 1,160kr. Stylish riverside hotel.

🏠 **Clarion Post** [17 D1] Drottningtorget 10; 031 61 90 00; e cl.post@ choice.se; w clarionpost.se; dbl from 1,880kr. Nordic comfort.

🏠 **Hotel Royal** [17 D1] Drottninggatan 67; 031 700 11 70; e info@hotel-royal.com; w hotel-royal.com; dbl from 1,795kr. Old-world grand.

🏠 **Hotel Vanilla** [17 B2] Kyrkogatan 38; 031 711 62 20; e info@ hotelvanilla.se; w hotelvanilla.se; dbl from 1,470kr. Mix of old & new.

TOP 5 RESTAURANTS

✗ **Bhoga** [17 B1] Norra Hamngatan 10; 031 13 80 18; e restaurang@ bhoga.se; w bhoga.se; 5-course tasting menu 600kr. The finest of Scandinavian ingredients. 1 Michelin star.

✗ **Bord 27** [14 E3] Haga Kyrkogata 14; 031 10 90 50; e info@bord27.se; w bord27.se; mains from 200kr. Family-owned restaurant with sensible prices.

✗ **Familjen** [14 F3] Arkivgatan 7; 031 20 79 79; e info@restaurangfamiljen. se; w restaurangfamiljen.se; mains from 225kr. Stylish European brasserie.

✗ **Gabriel** [14 F3] Feskekôrkan, Fisktorget 4; 031 13 90 51; e info@ restauranggabriel.se; w restauranggabriel.se; mains from 175kr. Succulent fresh fish.

✗ **Koka** [14 E3] Viktoriagatan 12; 031 701 79 79; e info@restaurangkoka. se; w restaurangkoka.se; 5-course tasting menu 695kr. Inventive modern Swedish. 1 Michelin star.

TOP 5 CAFÉS

☕ **Alkemisten** [14 F1] Gustaf Dalénsgatan 14; w alkemistenkaffebar.se. A favourite among coffee connoisseurs.

☕ **Bar Centro** [17 C2] Kyrkogatan 31; w barcentro.se. The best cappuccino in town.

☕ **Da Matteo** [17 B3] Magasinsgatan 17a; w damatteo.se. Urban chic with outdoor courtyard.

☕ **Kafe Magasinet** [14 D3] Tredje Långgatan 9; w kafemagasinet.se. Organic & fairtrade.

☕ **Rosenkaféet** [17 D1] Slussgatan 1; w rosenkafeet.se. Garden café surrounded by roses.

Exploring Gothenburg by boat is a fun thing to do. With departures from Kungsportsbron roughly every 20–30 minutes in summer (less frequently and not daily out of season), the open-topped **Paddan boats** (w stromma. se/paddan) make a 50-minute circuit (early April) of the city's canals before turning into the river and heading for Lilla Bommen harbour. Alternatively, boats depart from Lilla Bommen harbour every 90 minutes (early Jul–late Aug) for **Nya Älvsborg**, an island fortress in the Göta River, about 30 minutes west of the city centre. The fortification was built in the 17th century to defend the harbour and the city from Danish attack. A third option is the **Älvsnabben** public ferry, which operates all year and hops up and down the Göta River between Lilla Bommen and Klippan (close to the Stena Line Kiel terminal), offering great views of the city and the docks. Departures are every 30–60 minutes. Älvsnabben is included in the Västtrafik travelpass. For details, see box, page 18.

THE RIVERSIDE

From the Stadsmuseum, Norra Hamngatan continues west along the banks of Stora Hamnkanalen until it reaches the Göta River. Here, on the opposite bank of the canal, at **Stenpiren** (stone pier) [14 E2], there's a **monument** to New Sweden – a Swedish colony on the Delaware River in the United States which survived from 1638 to 1655. It was from piers here on the Göta River that ships once sailed to America with hundreds of emigrants on board.

MARITIMAN [14 E1] (Packhusplatsen 12; w maritiman.se; admission 140kr) Strolling north along the riverside towards the opera house, Göteborgsoperan, you'll quickly come to Maritiman, Gothenburg's fascinating maritime museum. It has no fewer than 13 vessels on display ranging from the huge cargo ship MS *Fryken*, which used to sail Lake Vänern and the North Sea, to the submarine *Nordkaparen*, once employed by the Swedish navy. While some of the ships are moored on the river, others are on display inside the range of buildings which run the length of the quayside.

LILLA BOMMEN HARBOUR [14 E1] Beyond the quayside opera house, the small harbour of yachts and other small boats is known as Lilla Bommen – *bommen* is Swedish for 'the barrier', and the harbour once marked the entrance from the river into one of Gothenburg's four canals, which ran the length of present-day Östra Hamngatan. Today the harbour is the place to come if you'd like to go **kayaking** – there's boat rental here from Point 65 Kayak Center (w kayaks.point65.com), located in the harbour itself. The graceful, four-masted ship moored just east of the harbour is the ***Barken Viking*** [14 E1] (w barkenviking.com), reputedly the biggest sailing ship ever built in Scandinavia. Originally, she served as a training ship for the Danish merchant navy, arriving in Gothenburg in 1950, where she now operates as a floating hotel.

UTKIKEN [14 F1] Towering over the *Barken Viking*, Utkiken (the lookout point) is a 22-storey office block whose red and white walls have made the structure a modern-day Gothenburg landmark – it's known colloquially as 'the lipstick' thanks to its garish stripes. Designed by the same Scottish architect, Ralph Erskine (1914–

The neo-Gothic Feskekörkan building (Kjell Holmner)

2005), who drew up plans for the Sydney Opera House, it's 86m high and offers arresting views of the city and its riverside location.

VOLVO MUSEUM [14 F1] (**w** volvomuseum.com; admission 100kr) Car enthusiasts and lovers of automobile memorabilia won't want to miss the Volvo museum in Gothenburg. From Lilla Bommen, it's a short walk across the bridge over the Göta River to Frihamnen, an area of wharfs and loading quays, where you can pick up Tram 5, 6 or 10 west to Eketrägatan. Here change on to Bus 32 towards Arendal and get off at the stop called Arendal Skans – then follow the signs for around 100m to the Volvo Museum (the bus operates on a ring-and-ride basis at weekends; call ☎ 031 788 0789 at least an hour before departure). Inside, you'll find an engaging exhibition dedicated to the history of Volvo (Latin for 'I roll') tracing development from the first car produced in 1927 to the present day. Over 100 vehicles and engines are on display: there's seemingly everything here from buses and trucks to aviation engines and classic cars.

BETWEEN THE CANALS

The grid of mostly pedestrian streets squeezed between Stora Hamnkanalen to the north and Rosenlundskanalen to the south is an ideal place to stroll and linger. Here, you'll find a great collection of shops as well as a range of tempting cafés and restaurants, in which to recharge your batteries. Keep an eye out, too, for **Antikhallarna** at Västra Hamngatan 6, a former bank and now Gothenburg's main antiques market.

DOMKYRKAN [17 B2] (Domkyrkan; Kungsgatan 37; **w** svenskakyrkan.se; free entry) Plonked between Västra Hamngatan and Korsgatan, Gothenburg's **cathedral** is unassuming in the extreme. It was built in 1815, replacing two former structures which were destroyed by fire despite the fact that they stood on some of the city's most waterlogged land. The present cathedral is constructed of yellow brick in classical style and its portico sports four giant Doric columns made of Scottish sandstone. Inside there are Empire and classical flourishes, though the main feature is the huge gilded altarpiece with plenty of angels – but no Jesus.

MAGASINSGATAN [17 A2] Two blocks west of Västra Hamngatan, Magasinsgatan is one of Gothenburg's most happening streets. Reaching all the way from Stora Hamnkanalen down to Rosenlundskanalen, this cobbled, pedestrian street has undergone a miraculous transformation in the past few years. Once one of the city's least desirable addresses, it's now a haven of **independent boutiques**, interior design stores and laidback **cafés**, not to mention the odd Michelin-starred restaurant and coffee roastery thrown in for good measure. While you're here, drop into **Da Matteo** (see box, page 19) – it's one of the city's favourite coffee shops and was even voted the best in the whole of Sweden in 2015 – or try **Strömmingsluckan** (w strommingsluckan.se), who sell delicious herring take-away; they're at Nos 17A and 17, respectively.

FESKEKÔRKAN (FISKTORGET) [14 E3] From the southern end of Magasinsgatan, it's a 5-minute walk west along the banks of Rosenlundskanalen to one of Gothenburg's most unusual-looking buildings: Feskekôrkan. Once you spot the neo-Gothic church-like building on the quayside, you'll soon understand where the unusual name originates: it does, indeed, mean 'fish church'. This fish market is undoubtedly the best place to buy fresh fish in the city: from catfish to crayfish – you name it, they've got it. The salmon alone comes in every variety you could imagine: cold-smoked, warm-smoked, cured, *gravad* – to name but a few. Naturally, you'll find one of the city's best fish restaurants here, too: **Gabriel** (see box, page 19 for details) – located upstairs in the small gallery.

KUNGSPORTSPLATSEN [17 C2] From Feskekôrkan, it's a pleasant 15-minute stroll back along Rosenlundskanalen east to the square which, to all intents and purposes, marks the southern edge of the city centre: Kungsportsplatsen. Named after one of the original entrances to the city, the King's Gate (Kungsport), which was demolished in the mid-1800s, the square is best known as the location for the glorious **Saluhallen foodhall** (w storasaluhallen.se; ⊕ 09.00–18.00 Mon–Fri & 09.00–16.00 Sat), which first opened its doors in 1839. Inside, the 40-odd stalls sell all manner of delicatessen

Gothenburg's Trädgårdsföreningen houses an impressive rose garden (Per Pixel Petersson)

items from all over the world as well as fresh meat and fish, while a handful of restaurants and cafés cater admirably to the city's hungry and thirsty shoppers.

TRÄDGÅRDSFÖRENINGEN [17 D2] (w tradgardsforeningen.se) Rest assured you're never going to be able to pronounce Trädgårdsföreningen – the Swedish name for this **ornamental garden**, located just across the Vallgraven canal from Kungsportsplatsen. Instead, be happy to know that the Garden Society of Gothenburg, as it's known in English, has been here since 1842 and has been delighting visitors ever since. In fact, in recent years the park has been lovingly restored to its former glory with the addition of woodland areas, flowerbeds and yet more roses. Indeed, the park boasts over 1,300 species of roses in the **Rosarium** [17 D1], which is one of the foremost rose gardens in the world, with no fewer than 2,500 roses in total. You'll find the inordinately popular café **Rosenkaféet** (see box, page 19) close by, surrounded by beautiful greenery and roses of every shade and fragrance, and oozing old-world charm. Wander into the magnificent **Palmhuset** [17 D2] as well while you're here – an ornate greenhouse made of cast iron and glass, it's modelled after London's Crystal Palace and contains an impressive host of palms, flowering trees and tropical plants.

AVENYN

Avenyn, or to give it its full, proper name, Kungsportsavenyn, is Gothenburg's answer to the Champs-Élysées. Inspired by the grand boulevards of Paris, Avenyn was the result of a town planning competition in 1861, when it was decided to develop the area south of Rosenlundskanalen as a residential area for the city's well-to-do. Avenyn winds gently uphill for roughly one kilometre from Kungsportsplatsen all the way to Götaplatsen square, from where there are good views back down the boulevard towards the city centre. Although many of the grand, former private homes have now been converted into shops and restaurants (of which Avenyn has aplenty) and their front gardens into pavements, palatial buildings still dominate its length – in particular, the ornate stucco work of Nos 16–22 never fails to catch the eye.

GÖTAPLATSEN [14 G3] As the location for Gothenburg's superb art museum, Konstmuseum, and Konserthuset, the city concert hall, Götaplatsen square is effectively the cultural heart of the city. However, before you indulge in art for art's sake, wander over to the sculpture which stands in the middle of the square: Carl Milles's giant, nude, bronze bodybuilder, **Poseidon** [14 G3]. Carl Milles (1875–1955) was one of Sweden's most prolific 20th-century sculptors and his work adorns many a public space up and down the country. However, when the 7m-tall Poseidon was unveiled to the attendant crowd one early September evening in 1931, the ample size of the figure's penis caused shock and outrage among the city's genteel ladyfolk, who called for Poseidon's manhood to be immediately downsized. Bowing to public pressure, Milles lopped off Poseidon's pride and joy, replacing it with the rather pathetically proportioned member you see today. However, Milles had the last laugh since, if you stand on the steps of the Konserthuset and view the statue sideways, you'll see that the enormous fish in Poseidon's hand does indeed appear to be a giant penis – hence, the statue is often known as Milles's revenge.

KONSTMUSEUM [14 G3] (Götaplatsen; w goteborgskonstmuseum.se; admission 60kr) No trip to Gothenburg is complete without a visit to the city's absorbing art museum, the vast Konstmuseum located at the top of Avenyn behind the Poseidon statue in Götaplatsen square. As it is the city's biggest and best museum, you should allow plenty of time to see the extensive collections here, which includes contemporary art as well as the excellent **Fürstenberg galleries** of early 20th-century Nordic art. However, before you head to the art galleries themselves on the upper floors, have a nose around the **Hasselblad Center**, immediately to the left of the entrance hall on the ground floor, where you'll find a fine and ever-changing exhibition of **Nordic photography**. Upstairs, you'll first come to the museum's collection of **European art** from the 15th to 17th centuries, which contains works by some of the great artists of the period: for example, Rembrandt, Rubens, Monet, Cézanne and Gauguin are all here. In the Swedish section, Carl Larsson (1853–1919) is well represented – look out for his *Little Susanne* in oil – and the monumental *Bringing Home the Body of Karl XII of Sweden* by Gustaf Cederström (1835–1933) portrays a band of wounded Swedish soldiers trudging through the snow, carrying the dead body of their king from Norway back to Sweden.

Fürstenberg Galleries

Continue up to the top floor of the museum for the Fürstenberg galleries, which contain a tremendous array of early 20th-century Scandinavian art and which are the real reason to make a visit to the museum. Nordic art from the turn of 19th century draws heavily on natural symbolism in its depictions: one popular theme is the blue, Nordic light of a long, summer evening.

Indeed, as you enter the galleries you'll come face to face with one of the most Swedish of all the paintings here: Richard Bergh's (1858–1911) floor-to-ceiling *Nordic Summer Evening*, which perfectly captures the spirit of the Swedish summer as a couple gaze dreamily over a lake from their veranda. Look out, too, for *Näcken* by Ernst Josephson (1851–1906), a vivid portrayal of the naked male water sprite, ever-prominent in Swedish folklore, who plays his fiddle so hauntingly that women and children from all around are lured to their deaths in his watery home.

The Gothenburg colourists

In 1907, Henry Matisse opened a painting academy in Paris which would later greatly influence art in Gothenburg. The school was attended by a number of Nordic artists, including **Tor Bjurström** (1888–1966) who became an influential teacher at the **Valand School of Fine Arts** in Gothenburg, where he was instrumental in introducing the French style of modern art to Sweden. His students became known as the **Gothenburg colourists** thanks to their flamboyant use of colour as a form of individual and distinctive expression. Together, the colourists developed a new tradition of Gothenburg painting which is today considered a separate genre within Swedish 20th-century art. You'll find some of their work within the Fürstenberg galleries: look out, in particular, for Tor Bjurström's *Harbour*, whose angular blocks interspersed with bold reds and blacks perfectly capture the mood of the port in Copenhagen.

KONSTHALL

[14 G3] (Götaplatsen 7; w konsthallen.goteborg.se) If you're longing for something more contemporary, head over to the Konsthall, right next door to the Konstmuseum, where you'll find an engaging collection of the latest work from some of Sweden's up-and-coming modern artists – what's more, admission is always free here.

RÖHSSKA MUSEET

[14 F3] (Vasagatan 37–39; w rohsska.se; admission 60kr) West of Avenyn on Vasagatan, you'll find Sweden's answer to London's famous Victoria and Albert Museum. The Röhsska Museet, named after the family of merchants who set it up, recounts the story of 150 years of Swedish and Scandinavian design, fashion and decorative art. As you wander around the museum, you'll spot a whole host of items which you'll recognise instantly, even as a non-Swede: the classic

LISEBERG AMUSEMENT PARK

[14 G3] (w liseberg.se; prices vary depending on which attractions you choose, which pass you choose & when you go; lengthy options on the website) If you walk for around 10–15 minutes northeast from Götaplatsen to Örgrytevägen 5, the screams will progressively get louder and louder until you arrive at Liseberg itself: Scandinavia's biggest **amusement park**.

The sheer array of rides, most notably the massive, wooden **rollercoaster**, 'Balder' (twice voted the best in the world in an international survey), which boasts speeds of 90km/h, is quite befuddling. Indeed, Liseberg specialises in rollercoasters – after 'Balder', try 'Valkyria', the longest dive coaster in Europe, featuring a vertical drop of 50m at a speed of 105km/h; or the hair-raising 'Helix', which turns upside-down no fewer than seven times, reaches a top speed of 100km/h and double launches at 4.3G.

Although the rides only operate between late April and early October and at Halloween (special events) and Christmas, Liseberg is also worth a look if you're in Gothenburg between mid-November and late December when the **Christmas market** is in full swing, selling handicrafts and presents.

Full details of events at the park are available online.

Liseberg is Scandinavia's biggest amusement park and holds a Christmas market every year
(Stefan Karlberg/ Liseberg)

Scandinavian design chairs you're no doubt familiar with from IKEA; the plain-glass vodka bottles emblazoned with the blue logo of Absolut; not to mention any number of mobile phones from Finland's NOKIA. Once you've had your fill of Nordic design, saunter up to the top floor to check out the 2m-tall Buddhas, which adorn an entire room, and peruse the Chinese and Japanese arts and crafts.

UNIVERSEUM [14 G3] (Södra Vägen 50; w universeum.se; admission 250kr mid-Jun–late Aug; rest of year 190kr) Next door to Liseberg, Universeum is Gothenburg's award-winning science and environment museum aimed predominantly at kids. With seven floors of fun and informative things to do and see, there's everything from tropical rainforests with monkeys to aquaria with sharks – even a mock-up of a space station.

VÄRLDSKULTURMUSEET [14 G4] (Södra Vägen 54; w www.varldskulturmuseet. se; admission free) True, Gothenburg has its fair share of museums, but if you're going to see just one or two of them, be sure to put Världskulturmuseet on your list. Not only has the building – complete with an enormous glass atrium – been awarded one of Sweden's top architectural prizes for creative design, but the Museum of World Culture, as it's called in English, hosts thought-provoking, informative and innovative exhibitions about world culture in its many fascinating forms. Presentations could feature anything from sex taboos in China to indigenous peoples in South America.

HAGA

Opposite Feskekôrkan on the southern side of Rosenlundskanalen, the district of Haga was established on the order of Queen Christina in the mid 17th century and was the first of the city's suburbs to be built. Between **Järntorget** in the west and **Handelshögskolan** (School of Economics) to the east, these rows of parallel streets fast became Gothenburg's main area of working-class housing and, indeed, the district had a somewhat chequered reputation for crime and vice during the 19th century. As part of the Social Democrats' out-with-the-old and in-with-the-new policy of the 1960s, the authorities drew up plans to totally demolish Haga; similar moves were afoot in Stockholm's working-class suburbs too. Thankfully, local opposition forced the plans to be dropped and, instead, the government implemented a programme of restoration to save some of the original houses from collapse. Following a major renovation in the 1980s, the area was completely spruced up and gentrified. Today, Haga is one of the city's most enjoyable quarters and a great place to see the attractive **wooden architecture** for which Gothenburg is justifiably known. Following a spate of fires during the 17th and 18th centuries, a ban was introduced on wooden houses of more than two storeys high, while stone buildings of several floors were equally impractical as they tended to sink into the boggy ground on which the city is built. Instead, a provincial governor hit upon the idea of building houses with a stone ground floor and timber storeys above. **Governor's houses** (*landshövdingehus*), as they became known, sprang up across Haga and today features as one of the district's defining attributes.

HAGA NYGATAN AND AROUND [14 E3] For a taste of Haga, take a leisurely stroll down pedestrianised Haga Nygatan, the main street in the district. It stretches over half a dozen blocks west from the university on Sprängkullsgatan and teems with

One of Gothenburg's two surviving
17th-century fortress towers in
Haga (Dick Gillberg)

independent shops selling everything from antiques and handicrafts to designer goods and vintage fashion items. As you meander your way past artsy stores, villagey cafés whose outdoor tables spill out on to the cobbles in summer, and the raft of excellent restaurants for which Haga is deservedly known, keep an eye out for the **wooden *landshövdingehus*,** often painted in subtle, pastel colours, which conspire to make this one of Gothenburg's most attractive areas. Don't miss, either, **Café Husaren** (No 24; **w** cafehusaren.se) at the university end of the street, which is reputed to serve the biggest and best *kanelbullar* (cinnamon buns) in town – the café itself is located in one of Haga's most ornate buildings, complete with original glass roof dating from the late 1800s. Close by at No 19, you'll find the popular leather shop **Haga Trätoffelfabrik** (**w** hagatratoffel.se), whose most sought-after item is the lowly clog (a popular working shoe for labourers in Scandinavia), though it also sells woollen sweaters and socks.

However, if you're looking for something altogether more alternative and bohemian, you'll find it at Haga Nygatan's western end: from here four parallel

SHOPPING IN GOTHENBURG

In line with Gothenburg's ranking as Sweden's second city, shopping opportunities in the city are plentiful and varied. Undoubtedly, the largest single collection of stores (around 200 in all) is found inside Nordstan, the giant **shopping mall** located opposite Centralstation (page 17). If you're looking for **interior design** items, or perhaps something a little **arty** or **alternative**, try the shops on Magasinsgatan (page 22) plus those in neighbouring Kyrkogatan, Kungsgatan and Södra Larmgatan. **T-shirts** emblazoned with Gothenburg or Sweden motifs are most readily found at one of the two tourist offices, either inside Nordstan or at Kungsportsplatsen 2. Good-quality **handicrafts** can be found at Kronhusbodarna at Postgatan 6–8. **Secondhand books** are for sale at Haga Nygatan 20 in Haga and also at Amerikagatan 4. New books and maps are readily found at Akademibokhandeln inside Nordstan. If you're after **delicatessen** items, try Saluhallen (page 22) in Kungsportsplatsen or Feskekôrkan (page 22) for something a little more fishy.

side streets known as **Första** (1st), **Andra** (2nd), **Tredje** (3rd) and **Fjärde** (4th) **Långgatan** contain a range of off-beat stores, as well as restaurants, cafés and wine bars. The pick of the streets is probably Andra Långgatan, which boasts an eclectic range of urban fashion stores, record shops and alternative cafés.

SKANSPARKEN AND SKANSEN KRONAN [14 D3] From Haga Nygatan, a short stroll south down either Västra Skansgatan or Kaponjärgatan leads to Skansparken, not really a park, more a steep tree-covered **knoll** that is the location for Skansen Kronan (w skansenkronan.se), one of Gothenburg's two surviving 17th-century **fortress towers** and probably Sweden's best preserved. With walls of granite and gneiss measuring around 5m thick, the tower was key to the city's defences against possible Danish attack from the south, though, in reality, Skansen Kronan was never attacked and the 20-odd cannons were never used. Today, the tower is in private ownership and the real reason to venture up here is to take in the great views back over the city, the harbour and the river.

LINNÉ

South of Haga, the trendy café and restaurant district of Linné is centred on **Linnégatan** [14 D3–4], the main thoroughfare which wends its way for around 1km from Järntorget (beside the Stena Line Denmark terminal) down towards Linnéplatsen square and **Slottsskogen city park** [14 C/D4], the vast expanse of parkland on the city's southern fringes. Although it's often marked as Olivedal on some maps, this area is more commonly known as Linné and is named after Swedish botanist Carl von Linné (1707–88), who invented the binomial classification of plants and animals still in use today (eg: *Homo sapiens*). He visited Gothenburg in 1746 as part of his research journey across West Sweden. The **houses** that line Linnégatan are unusually tall, which tends to give the impression that Linnégatan is rather narrow. True, that image is often compounded by the busy traffic heading in and out of town, but don't be put off: it's still a pleasant place for a stroll and you may well find yourself tempted inside one or two of the district's many excellent eating and drinking establishments as you wander. Many of the houses along Linnégatan date from the early 1900s, though some are much more recent additions, built during the 1980s but carefully designed to resemble their predecessors. Indeed, as people began moving into these new homes, they created a ready market for

The southern district of Linné is renowned for its laid-back café culture (Beatrice Törnros)

Since spring 2015, Gothenburg has had a new sandy beach, sauna and public pool right on the riverside in Frihamnen where development of the former docks has been happening apace. Full details are at w alvstaden. goteborg.se/jubileumsparken. Another option is to head to one of the islands in the archipelago if you're looking to sunbathe and swim – we've given full details in the *Gothenburg Archipelago* chapter (page 31). However, if you'd prefer to stay on the mainland, why not try the *kallbadhus* (cold-water bathhouse) at **Saltholmen** (w saltholmenskallbadhus.se; ⏁ 09.00–19.00 daily; admission 60kr), 11km southwest of the city centre and easily reached by tram. Founded in 1908, the bathing house and adjoining **nude beaches**, both sandy and rocky, are as popular today as ever – there's one section for men, one for women and one for both sexes. The entire site, which also features a sauna, is open from May to mid-September. Remember, though, this is a naked bathing area, so leave your swimwear behind.

the many cafés and restaurants which now line Linnégatan; during the summer months, many offer delightful outdoor terraces located in the former front gardens of the grand old houses they occupy.

SLOTTSSKOGEN CITY PARK [14 C4] (w goteborg.se/slottsskogen) Covering an impressive 140ha, Slottsskogen is every Gothenburger's favourite open space – people come here to jog, stroll, picnic or simply to enjoy the peace and quiet of this green oasis within the city. Originally, this roughly circular expanse of **parkland** was a forest which belonged to the Älvsborg fortress. By the late 1800s, though, the city was already encroaching on the edges of the forest, so a local merchant took the initiative to create today's Slottsskogen, a city park modelled on an English garden, complete with neatly tended lawns and flower beds. In addition to the grassy expanses which are very popular for summer picnics, there's also a **zoo** with a small collection of animals from the Nordic countries such as elk and seals and an **open-air heritage centre** showcasing old wooden cottages from the various regions of Sweden. If you're here around late May and early June, don't miss the stunning azaleas which are in full bloom at this time of year. Although the plant is not native to Sweden, it grows well here and is present in such numbers in one particular area of the park that it's been dubbed 'azalea valley'.

BOTANICAL GARDENS [14 D4] (w botaniska.se; admission voluntary 20kr for the gardens; greenhouses obligatory 20kr) Just across Carl Skottbergs gata from Slottsskogen city park, Gothenburg's Botanical Gardens are one of the largest in Europe, containing 16,000 species of plants in various greenhouses and gardens. Not only do the gardens contain the largest collection of tropical orchids in Sweden, but, more significantly, they are also home to one of the rarest trees in the world: the enigmatic **Easter Island tree**. The tree, *Sophora toromiro*, which is related to the Japanese pagoda tree, was grown from seeds brought back in the 1950s from Easter Island in the South Pacific by Norwegian explorer Thor Heyerdahl. It is now extinct in its native habitat and would indeed be extinct worldwide were it not for the efforts of the botanical gardens in Gothenburg. Its yellow flowers bloom in spring, though, sadly, all efforts to further reproduce new trees from seeds have failed.

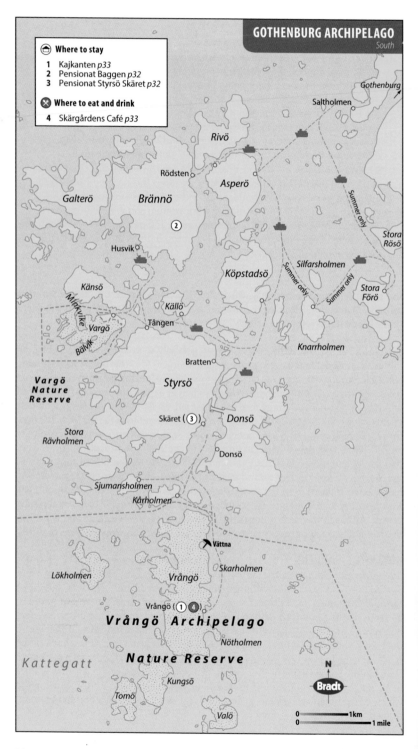

GOTHENBURG ARCHIPELAGO
South

Where to stay

1 Kajkanten *p33*
2 Pensionat Baggen *p32*
3 Pensionat Styrsö Skäret *p32*

Where to eat and drink

4 Skärgårdens Café *p33*

Gothenburg

Saltholmen

Rivö

Rödsten

Asperö

Galterö *Brännö*

②

Husvik

Stora Rösö

Silfarsholmen

Köpstadsö

Summer only

Känsö

Källö

Stora Förö

Minkvike

Vargö Tången

Bälvik

Knarrholmen

Bratten

Vargö Nature Reserve *Styrsö*

Stora Rävholmen

Skäret (③) *Donsö*

Donsö

Sjumansholmen

Kårholmen

Vättna

Lökholmen *Vrångö* Skarholmen

Vrångö (① ④)

Vrångö Archipelago

Nötholmen

Kattegatt *Nature Reserve*

N

Kungsö

Bradt

Tomö

0 ————— 1km

0 ————— 1 mile

Valö

2

Gothenburg Archipelago

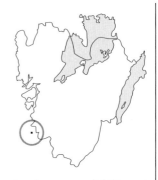

No matter whether you arrive in Gothenburg by ferry or by plane, you can't fail to spot the array of coastal islands that lie just off the city's southwestern peninsula. Both the southern and northern parts of the archipelago are a favourite summer playground for holidaying Gothenburgers – and for good reason. Not only are the islands easy and inexpensive to reach, they offer some of the city's best beaches and sunbathing opportunities. Perhaps best of all, though, many of the islands are car-free: transport is instead by bike or motorised three-wheeler mopeds which are used for deliveries. Accordingly, the pace of life out in the archipelago is enviably sedate – a trip to any of the islands offers a rare chance to slow down and take it easy: cycle down winding lanes decked with wild roses, stroll through leafy woodlands or lay out your towel on the smooth rocks that line these shores and soak up the summer sunshine. Connections to the mainland are frequent and reliable, making it perfectly feasible to spend the night in the archipelago in a hotel or guesthouse should you choose to do so. There's more information about all parts of the archipelago at **w** goteborg.com/en/archipelago.

BRÄNNÖ AND GALTERÖ

Unlike the other islands in the archipelago, Brännö has never earned its fortunes from fishing. Instead, the islanders have always farmed the relatively productive

The Gothenburg archipelago is dotted with tiny islands (Jorma Valkonen)

arable land that proliferates on the eastern side; today, sheep graze in fields in the middle of the island. Brännö is also known for its strong associations with Swedish **folk music** – every Thursday evening in summer, there's dancing and music on the quayside in Husvik, the most southerly of the two jetties served by the ferries from Saltholmen. There's a pleasant **walk** of a couple of hours or so starting from Brännö's wooden church in the centre of the village: take Galterövägen northwest across to the neighbouring island of Galterö (also used for sheep grazing), where there are great views of the Kattegatt and the sea approaches to Gothenburg, and follow the circular walking path which leads around Galterö. There's overnight accommodation on Brännö, **Pensionat Baggen** – it's bookable through Brännö Värdshus (**w** brannovardshus.se; dbl room 1,490kr) and has its own bakery and beer brand.

STYRSÖ AND DONSÖ

Located in the central section of the archipelago, pastoral **Styrsö** is a firm favourite. With a population of around 1,600 people (which doubles in summer), it's also one of the bigger islands and consequently offers a wide range of landscapes: you'll find everything here from undulating flower meadows and deciduous woodland, to smooth rocky outcrops and fine sandy beaches. Indeed, one of the main reasons people come here is to visit the child-friendly **Brattenbadet beach**, barely 5 minutes from the main ferry jetty.

However, Styrsö's real charms can be found by **cycling** along the quiet country lanes which weave across the island, perhaps stopping for a picnic down on the coast. The smooth rocks on the northwest coast of Styrsö are ideal for anyone seeking total solitude – get here by cycling west through the main village bound for Sandvik and then turning into Lunnevägen. Leave your bike here and clamber up over the rocks in front of you heading for the western shoreline – here you can **sunbathe** and **swim** totally undisturbed, enjoying the wide-open views of the sea. Overnight accommodation is available at **Pensionat Styrsö Skäret** (**w** pensionatskaret.se; dbl room from 1,795kr), which also serves lunch and offers free bike rental for guests.

Linked to Styrsö by bridge, neighbouring **Donsö** is an altogether busier sort of place where life revolves around the bustling harbour. However, on the eastern side of the island behind the **church**, there's a handful of small **sandy bays**, which are Donsö's main attraction.

VARGÖ

If you're looking to commune with nature, Vargö is for you. Declared a **nature reserve** in 1986, this rocky island of bare heathland is pretty much as far west in the archipelago as you can go, and, consequently, it takes the full force of the wind as it blasts in off the Kattegatt. One of the most sheltered areas is **Bälvik**, on the south coast, where there's a wonderful sandy little **cove**, ideal for a dip; a **walking trail** leads here from the ferry jetty. Vargö is renowned for its wide diversity of flora: at **Minkviken** on the north coast you'll find large expanses of sea lavender whose blue-violet flowers are in bloom during July and August. Elsewhere, particularly at Bälvik, there's sea kale, sea rocket, thrift and sea campion – all four plants are characteristic of the Swedish west coast. From Bälvik, the walking trail continues west across the island where the vegetation is considerably sparser; here Vargö shows its more elemental face with bare expanses of granite.

> **GETTING TO THE ISLANDS**
>
> Ferries operated by Styrsöbolaget (w styrsobolaget.se) run from Saltholmen, 11km southwest of Gothenburg city centre, to the various islands of the southern archipelago. Twice-daily services operate year-round from Stenpiren in the city centre, too. Saltholmen itself is easily reached by Tram 11 or alternatively by express Bus 114 from the Nils Ericson Terminalen. The ferries are free if you have a Västtrafik travelpass (for details, see box, page 18). Otherwise, buy your ticket on board the boats using either cash or credit card (60kr return). Typical journey times from Saltholmen are Brännö (20mins), Styrsö (25mins), Vargö (40mins) and Vrångö (50mins).

VRÅNGÖ

A large island but with a population of just 400, Vrångö has the best **beaches** of all the islands in the archipelago. Since it lies towards the southern end of the chain, Vrångö takes a little longer to reach from Saltholmen than the other islands, but it more than repays the little extra effort it takes to get there. From the ferry jetty, there are two circular walking paths to choose from, each going through a **nature reserve** and about 2.5km in length. The southern trail leads past the small peninsula, **Nötholmen**, which is where you'll find a wonderful lagoon with a great **sandy beach** that's ideal for swimming. The path continues to the west coast, where you'll find countless small **creeks** and **inlets** which are perfectly suited to swimming and sunbathing; the path then swings inland and heads back towards the village. Alternatively, the northern trail leads from the ferry jetty to two of Vrångö's other beaches: the first, opposite the islet of **Skarholmen** just offshore, features a large grassy area (great for picnics and barbecues) and a glorious sandy strand. The second beach, **Vättna**, a little further on, boasts an even larger stretch of perfect golden sand. Should you wish to continue walking, the trail swings inland from the beach, heading for Vrångö's west coast before finally looping round and leading back into the village again. For a *fika* after your walk, head to **Skärgårdens Café** (w skargardenscafevrango.se) for refreshments located right beside the ferry jetty. There's also the chance to spend the night on the island at **Kajkanten** (w kajkantenvrango.se) on the western side of the island at Hamnväg 24.

Gothenburg Archipelago VRÅNGÖ

2

Reached by ferry, the southern islands are car free.
Pictured here: Vrångö (Emil Fagander)

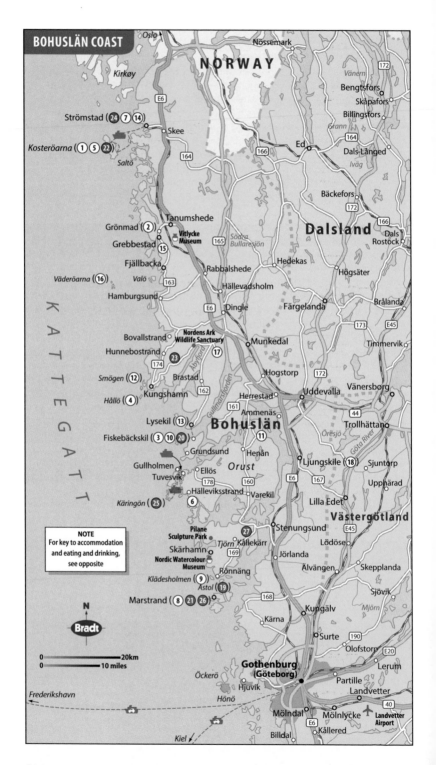

BOHUSLÄN COAST

Oslo
Nössemark
NORWAY
Vänern   172
Kirkøy
Bengtsfors
Skåpafors
E6   Billingsfors
Strömstad (24)(7)(14)   Grann
Skee
Ed   164
Kosteröarna (1)(5)(22)   Dals-Långed
164   166   Iväg
Saltö

Bäckefors
172

Tanumshede
Grönmad (2)   Dalsland   166
Vitlycke   Dals
Museum   165   Södra   Rostock
Grebbestad (15)   Bullaresjön
Fjällbacka   Hedekas
Rabbalshede   Högsäter
Väderöarna (16)   Valö   163   Hällevadsholm
Hamburgsund   Brålanda
E6   Dingle   Färgelanda
173   E45
Nordens Ark
Bovallstrand Wildlife Sanctuary
Hunnebostrand (23)   (17) Munkedal   Timmervik
174   Abyfjord
Smögen (12)   Brastad   Hogstorp   172
Hållö (4)   Kungshamn   162   Vänersborg
Herrestad   Uddevalla
161   Ammenäs   44
Lysekil (13)   Trollhättan
Bohuslän   Öresjö
Fiskebäckskil (3)(10)(20)   (11)
Grundsund   Henån   Ljungskile (18) Sjuntorp
Gullholmen   Ellös   Orust   E6   167   Upphärad
Tuvesvik   178   160
Hälleviksstrand Varekil   Lilla Edet
Käringön (25)   (6)   Västergötland
NOTE   Pilane   Stenungsund   E45
For key to accommodation Sculpture Park (27)
and eating and drinking, Skärhamn Tjörn Kållekärr   Lödöse
see opposite   Nordic Watercolour 169   Jörlanda
Museum   Älvängen   Skepplanda
Klädesholmen (9)   Rönnäng
Astol (19)   Sjövik
Marstrand (8)(21)(26)   168
Kungälv   Mjörn
Kärna
N
Surte   190
Bradt
Olofstorp   E20
0   20km
0   10 miles   Gothenburg
Öckerö   (Göteborg)   Lerum
Frederikshavn   Hjuvik   Partille
Hönö   Landvetter
Mölndal Mölnlycke   Landvetter
E6   Airport   40
Kiel   Billdal   Kållered

KATTEGATT

3

Bohuslän Coast

Without a doubt, the Bohuslän coast is one of Sweden's most enchanting and alluring regions. As you'd expect, the landscape is dominated by the sea: this is a region of rocky bluffs, cliffs, islands and skerries which stretches for 160km from Gothenburg to the Norwegian border. Yet what makes this deeply indented coastline, punctuated with no fewer than 8,000 islands, so special is the unusual colouring of the rock – pink. Known as **Bohus granite**, the rock bears a distinctly pink hue and is found extensively between Fjällbacka and Lysekil, often running in linear formation a little off the coast. Naturally, small fishing communities grew up around the numerous natural harbours and herring, in particular, remained the region's lifeblood until the early 1900s.

Today, though, Bohuslän is known for its succulent **seafood**: mussels, oysters, lobsters, langoustines, crabs and prawns all thrive in the deep, cold and exceptionally clean waters off the Swedish west coast. The cold waters cause the crustaceans to grow more slowly than in warmer climates, which consequently produces an exceptional taste. A trip up the coast offers the opportunity to see and sample mussels and oysters in their natural habitat on board a '**seafood safari**'; alternatively, take to the water in a **sea kayak** and explore the coast's uninhabited islets and islands at your own pace; go **walking**; or head out to any of the larger islands for a spot of **island hopping**, or simply **cycle** along quiet country lanes out to the beach and laze in the summer sunshine.

Inland, Bohuslän offers a range of diversions: everything from stunning **Bronze Age rock carvings** – the greatest concentration of carvings located anywhere in Scandinavia – to a superb wildlife sanctuary and marine park housing some of the world's most **endangered species**. Quite simply, Bohuslän is West Sweden at its best.

BOHUSLÄN COAST

🏠 Where to stay

1 Ekenäs Koster *p54*
2 Everts Sjöbod *p51*
3 Gullmarsstrand *p43*
4 Hållö youth hostel *p47*
5 Kostergården *p55*
6 Lådfabriken *p40*
7 Laholmen *p52*
8 Marstrands Havshotell *p42*
9 Salt och Sill *p42*
10 Slipens Hotell & Pensionat *p43*
11 Slussens Pensionat *p40*
12 Smögens Hafvsbad *p42*
13 Strandflickorna Havshotell *p42*
14 Strömstad Spa *p52*
15 Tanumstrand *p51*
16 Väderöarnas Värdshus *p49*
17 Vann Spa *p47*
18 Villa Sjötorp *p42*

❌ Where to eat and drink

19 Åstols Café *p39*
20 Brygghuset *p42*
   Everts Sjöbod (see 2)
21 Grand Hotel Marstrand *p42*
   Gullmarsstrand (see 3)
   Hållö youth hostel (see 4)
22 Kosters Trädgårdar *p42*
23 Lyckans Stenugnsbageri *p48*
24 Rökeriet i Strömstad *p52*
   Salt och Sill (see 9)
25 Simsons Prästgård *p41*
26 Societetshuset *p36*
27 Sundsby Säteri *p39*
   Väderöarnas Värdshus (see 16)
   Vatten (see Nordic Watercolour Museum) *p42*
   Villa Sjötorp (see 18)
   Vitlycke Museum café (see Vitlycke Museum) *p51*

MARSTRAND

A delightful holiday island with no cars, more yachts than you can ever imagine and the imposing stone fortress **Carlsten** to top it all off: this is Marstrand, a firm west coast favourite and sailing centre, about 50km northwest of Gothenburg and linked to the mainland by a 5-minute ferry ride. Founded in the 1200s by Norwegian king Haakon Haakonsson, Marstrand only became Swedish, like the rest of Bohuslän, in 1658 with the signing of the Treaty of Roskilde. Over the centuries it owed its fortunes to both **herring** and the establishment of an autonomous **free port** until times changed and the town became eclipsed by burgeoning Gothenburg. Marstrand reinvented itself as a fashionable **bathing resort** in the 1800s, even winning the patronage of King Oscar II who regularly visited during the summer months. Today, wandering around the cobbled streets and alleyways, popping into the many handicraft and clothing shops, admiring the pretty wooden houses and stopping for a cup of coffee and a cinnamon bun on the quayside are all an agreeable way to spend a morning or afternoon in Marstrand.

MARSTRANDS KYRKA (w svenskakyrkan.se (non-specific site); free entry) One block inland from the quayside on Kyrkogatan and dating from the 1200s, **Marstrand church** was originally attached to a Franciscan monastery and, accordingly, bears more than a passing resemblance to the low, squat churches common around the Mediterranean. Inside behind the altar, there's a **crucifix** from the 1400s and a series of ten **paintings** by Gothenburg artist Eric Grijs of scenes from the biblical History of the Heart. Just outside the church, at the junction of Långgatan and Kungsgatan, Marstrand's idyllic main square, **Torget**, is dominated by a massive silver poplar tree which was planted in 1866.

SOCIETETSHUSET (w societetshuset.se) The pompous wedding-cake-like wooden building at the northern end of Långgatan overlooking the sea is Societetshuset. It was here that King Oscar II entertained the great and the good during his summer stays in Marstrand in the late 1880s and 1890s. Today, it's a classy summer-only **restaurant** and entertainment facility.

CARLSTEN FORTRESS (w carlsten.se; admission 95kr) Built by order of King Carl Gustav X following Sweden's acquisition of Bohuslän, the massive **Carlsten fortress**

The easiest way to get around the coast is by **car**. Distances between points of interest are quite manageable: Gothenburg to Marstrand is 47km; Lysekil to Fjällbacka is 56km; and Vitlycke to Strömstad is 35km, for example. By public transport, connections up and down the coast can be somewhat time-consuming. Trains run between Gothenburg and Strömstad and buses operate out to the coast from various stations along its length. Elsewhere, the bus network is relatively comprehensive. Ferries link several offshore islands with the mainland – full details are in the text. All timetables are available at **w** vasttrafik.se.

served for centuries as a bastion against Danish invasion. Embarrassingly for the Swedes, it fell to the enemy on the only two occasions it was attacked – hard to believe when you view the seemingly impregnable walls, reinforced by a moat and drawbridge, which soar up above the town it was designed to defend. **Guided tours** of the fortress give a chilling insight into the harsh conditions endured by the prisoners inside; some drew paintings in their own blood, while others slowly wore away the stone of the windowsill of their cells by constantly tapping their fingers. Best known of the inmates was **Lasse-Maja**, a kind of Swedish Robin Hood, who, dressed as a woman, stole money from the rich and hapless.

STRANDVERKET KONSTHALL (**w** strandverket.se; admission 70kr) Down on the quayside at Hamngatan 56, you'll find the impressive private art gallery, **Strandverket Konsthall**. Inside the sturdy stone walls of the fortress's former cannon defences, you'll find a terrific collection of paintings, photographs, digital art and sculptures. There are always two exhibitions running concurrently; see website for details.

AROUND THE ISLAND A 5km **walking trail** leads around the island, offering a perfect chance to swim and sunbathe on the way – reckon on around 90 minutes to complete the walk. On the southern side of the island at **Svarte Udde** there's official segregated **nude bathing** for both men and women. On the north and east coasts you'll find a further three **bathing areas** spread across a series of flat rocks; steps enable access into the sea. Two small **beaches** can also be found just west of the Konsthall.

Carlsten fortress dominates the Marstrand skyline (Jonas Ingman)

Bohuslän Coast MARSTRAND

TJÖRN

A triangular-shaped island immediately north of Marstrand, though only reached by doubling back to the mainland and routing via Stenungsund, Tjörn (roughly pronounced 'shurn') has two quintessentially West Swedish attractions aplenty: watercolours and herring. Admittedly, not an immediately obvious combination, but an engaging one nonetheless.

NORDIC WATERCOLOUR MUSEUM (Södra Hamnen 6; w akvarellmuseet.org; admission 100kr) Down by the water's edge in Tjörn's unassuming main town, **Skärhamn**, the Nordic Watercolour Museum is really the last thing you'd expect to find here. Yet, benefiting from its striking waterside location, this is somehow the perfect location for a museum dedicated to changing exhibitions by some of the world's greatest watercolour painters, though the focus is on artists from the Nordic countries. The bright and airy seafood restaurant inside the museum, **Vatten Restaurang & Kafé** (w restaurangvatten.com; see box, page 42, for details), is worth a look for its stunning location alone.

PILANE SCULPTURE PARK (w pilane.org; admission 100kr) Annoyingly poorly signposted (get exact directions from the website), yet definitely worth the effort to reach, Pilane is an open-air sculpture park near the village of **Kållekärr**. The site, which covers around 8ha of tussocky grassland and rocky outcrops and is home to flocks of grazing sheep, was used as a burial ground during the Iron Age and contains graves over 2,000 years old. This curious combination of ancient and modern gives Pilane its very individual character; there are generally around 10–15 pieces of **modern art** and **sculptures** on display at any one time between mid-May and the end of September. Outside this period, the site is still open but there is no art on display.

Imposing sculptures and modern art are on display in the summer at Pilane open-air sculpture park (Roger Borgelid)

KLÄDESHOLMEN Linked to the mainland by a small bridge, Klädesholmen is an island of lovely wooden cottages set on steep inclines. Across Sweden it's known as the home of **herring**, and, although the number of producers has dwindled over the years, there are still three factories left that operate commercially under the name of Klädesholmen Seafood, producing over half of Sweden's supplies of *matjessill* (soused herring). It's here, too, that you'll find Sweden's first floating hotel and restaurant: **Salt och Sill** (w saltosill.se; see box, page 42). The hotel offers compact rooms decked out in maritime colours and styles right on the water (you can swim from right outside your room), and the restaurant serves the best herring for miles around and comes highly recommended.

SUNDSBY SÄTERI (**w** sundsbygardscafe.se) At the northern end of Tjörn, Sundsby Säteri is a graceful and stately **manor house** dating from the 16th century. Signposted off Route 160 between Stenungsund and Orust (west of Myggenäs), the manor house operates as a delightful **café and restaurant** (see website above for details) serving plenty of organic and locally sourced produce; there's also a farm shop on site. The main building is set in a leafy park containing a wide variety of flowers and trees, most impressively a 900-year-old knotty and rather hollow oak tree, where there's also an easy hiking trail. During the summer months, there's often a programme of outdoor theatre and music events.

ÅSTOL

The small island of Åstol typifies many aspects of the west coast with its uncrowded and unhurried atmosphere, small harbour, one single shop and a cosy bed and breakfast. In addition, there's a well-known and much-appreciated smokehouse which even puts on live music events, too. Though many locals simply sail over to Åstol in their private boats for a bite of lunch or a leisurely day out, the island is also connected to the mainland by a public ferry sailing from Rönnäng on Tjörn (times available on **w** vasttrafik.se). Check out Åstols Café, too, while you're here for an unmissable *fika*. It's perfectly located, right in the harbour, at Hamnvägen 6.

A bird's-eye view of the small island of Åstol (Jonas Ingman)

The tiny islet of Grundsund is home to one of Sweden's oldest fishing villages (Åsa Dahlgren)

ORUST

A centre for boatbuilding since Viking times, the island of Orust is bare on its windward coasts, yet has forest right up to its eastern shores. Cycling is a popular activity on the island and bikes can be hired from the waterside **Slussens Pensionat** (w slussenspensionat.se) in the village of Slussen, where there's often live musical performances and a great place to spend the night. Stylish to a T, another glorious place to savour the sweeping vistas of the west coast is **Lådfabriken** (w ladfabriken.eu) at Edshultshall; this former fish factory boasts picture windows just above the shoreline. Orust is pretty enough but there are other attractions just offshore, too: the tiny islet of Gullholmen is one of Sweden's oldest fishing villages, whereas Käringön island is quite simply the most beguiling place on the whole Swedish west coast and is not to be missed.

GULLHOLMEN AND HÄRMANÖ Passenger-only ferries leave for Gullholmen from Tuvesvik, 7km west of Ellös, and take just a quarter of an hour to sail across to the car-free island, which can trace its history back to the 13th century. The village, which has a substantial church surrounded by a dense huddle of red-and-white wooden homes, is predominantly located on the tiny island of Gullholmen, though it does spill over a small footbridge to the adjoining island of Härmanö, which is predominantly a nature reserve where birds nest undisturbed beneath smooth granite rocks and a number of rare plants flourish. Härmanö is known for its fissured bedrock which is known locally as 'hell's corridor'.

KÄRINGÖN No visit to West Sweden is complete without a trip to Käringön, the most enchanting of all the region's villages. Measuring a mere 1km wide and 1km long, this postcard-perfect island village charms each and every one of its visitors – the glorious jumble of timber houses beautifully painted in any number of subtle pastel shades, red wooden fishing shacks, outhouses and immaculately kept gardens has changed little over the past 150 years. Amble along the narrow pathways and lanes, bedecked in summer with wild roses, and you'll soon understand why this unspoilt little village is so special. Settlement here dates back to 1596 when the first families from Orust moved out to the island to fish; herring booms in later years saw the population rise to over 650. The village church dates from 1796 and it was here that the fiery preacher,

SEA KAYAKING ON THE BOHUSLÄN COAST

The waters off the Bohuslän coast are ideally suited to sea kayaking since there are no strong currents or tides and, during the summer months, are relatively warm. All kinds of tours are available, catering for everyone from the beginner to the enthusiast. Indeed, there are several operators located up and down the coast; for example **Upplevelsebolaget** in Uddevalla (w upplevelsebolaget.com), and **Nautopp** (w nautopp.se) and **Skärgårdsidyllen** (w skargardsidyllen.se) in Grebbestad, who operate from three points along the coast. Or, try **Kajaktiv** (w kajaktiv.se) who run guided tours in southern Bohuslän and rent out kayaks on **Tjörn**.

However, one of the best places to go sea kayaking in Bohuslän is from **Grundsund**, 6km southwest of Fiskebäckskil (page 43), at the western tip of Skaftö island. The offshore archipelago here acts as a windbreak, reducing waves and making kayaking generally smoother and more fun. Daily from May to October (advance booking required in May, September and October), you can hire kayaks from the quay in Grundsund for anything from a couple of hours to several days, taking tents and sleeping bags with you for some serious exploration. Tours can either take you out into the archipelago or, more adventurously, around the whole of Skaftö. Handy beginners' courses are also available to help you get to grips with kayak and paddle. Full details of tours and prices are available at w balanspunkten.nu and at w vastsverige.com/en/nature-experiences/paddling.

Paddle the peaceful corners of the Bohuslän coast on a sea kayaking tour (Henrik Trygg)

August Simson (1815–1900), delivered his highly moralistic sermons from 1850 to 1900; during his time on the island he outlawed dancing, smoking and, naturally, drinking, and was responsible for closing down several inns which served alcohol. His grave can be seen in the village churchyard. Opposite the church, the ornate vicarage dating from 1877, known as **Simsons Prästgård**, opens as a summer café and restaurant (w simsons.nu; 3-course menu for 495kr) complete with a tempting, shady garden. From the vicarage it's a short stroll following the north coast to the pilot lookout station in the far northwestern corner of the island where there are good views back across the sea to the mainland. Accommodation is available at **Hotel Käringön** (w karingon.se). **Ferries** sail to Käringön from Tuvesvik; timetables are available at w vasttrafik.se. In summer there are separate departures for Käringön; in winter the same boat serves both Gullholmen and Käringön.

TOP 5 PLACES TO STAY *Map, page 34*
Prices refer to high season.

🏠 **Marstrands Havshotell** Varvskajen 2, Marstrand; ☎0303 24 02 00;
e hej@marstrand.se; w marstrands.se; dbl 2,295kr. Chi-chi spa resort.

🏠 **Salt och Sill** Klädesholmen; ☎0304 67 34 80; e info@saltosill.se;
w saltosill.se; dbl 2,490kr. Floating hotel & excellent restaurant.

🏠 **Smögens Hafvsbad** Hotellgatan 26, Smögen; ☎05 23 668 450; e info@
smogenshafvsbad.se; w smogenshafvsbad.se; dbl from 1,690kr.

🏠 **Strandflickorna Havshotell** Turistgatan 13, Lysekil; ☎05 23 797 50;
e info@strandflickorna.se; w strandflickorna.se; dbl from 1,495kr. Old-world
charm.

🏠 **Villa Sjötorp** Sjötorpsvägen 5, Ljungskile; ☎0522 20174; e info@
villasjotorp.se; w villasjotorp.se; dbl from 1,998kr. Historic hotel.

TOP 5 PLACES TO EAT *Map, page 34*

✖ **Brygghuset** Fiskebäckskilsvägen 28, Fiskebäckskil; ☎05 23 222 22;
e info@brygghusetkrog.se; w brygghusetkrog.se; mains from 195kr.
Waterside dining in a stunning location.

✖ **Grand Hotel Marstrand** Rådhusgatan 2, Marstrand; ☎0303 603 22;
e info@grandmarstrand.se; w grandmarstrand.se. Mains from 295kr. Old-
world elegance overlooking the sea.

✖ **Kosters Trädgårdar** Sydkoster; ☎05 26 205 99; e info@kosterstradgardar.se;
w kosterstradgardar.se; mains from around 200kr. Organic treats.

✖ **Vatten Restaurang & Kafé** Södra hamen 6, Skärhamen; ☎0304 67 00
87; e bokning@restaurangvatten.se; w restaurangvatten.com; mains from
175kr. Inside the Nordic Watercolour Museum (page 38).

✖ **Villa Sjötorp** Sjötorpsvägen 5, Ljungskile; ☎0522 201 74; e info@
villasjotorp.se; w villasjotorp.se; mains around 298kr. Classic seafood dishes
are a speciality.

*While Bohuslän is known for
its succulent seafood, herring –
historically the region's lifeblood
– also features on the menu
(Jonas Ingman)*

Käringön's beaches Amazingly for such a small island, Käringön has no fewer than eight beaches, though none are classically sandy. All but two are located on the south coast and reached by walking paths from the village. At the island's southern tip there's are two beaches of smooth rocks, **Familjebadet** and **Friluftsbadet**; around the headland there are two separate-gender **nude beaches** located inside a weather-beaten *kallbadhus* (cold-water bathhouse); further east there's a children's beach, **Barnbadet**, then **Knoden**, which offers one of the easiest access points into the sea. Further east, **Tanternas vik** is a women-only nude beach, and, in the village itself, **Ö-viken**, with pontoons, has two bathing areas, one of which is suitable for children.

FISKEBÄCKSKIL

On the southern shore of Gullmarsfjorden, the small village of Fiskebäckskil is worth a stop for its inordinately cute **wooden houses**, which perch on rocky outcrops above the fjord, and its **church** from 1772. The church's interior bears luxuriant flourishes, such as etched mirrors with hand-carved wooden frames, all paid for by one of Bohuslän's grand dames, landowner Margareta Huidtfeldt (1608–83). Whilst here, look in the churchyard for the unadorned **grave** of Fiskebäckskil's most famous son, artist Carl Wilhelmson (1866–1928), whose work captures local life at the end of the 19th century. More unusually, the cemetery also contains the shared grave of a German soldier and an English naval officer who died together in the Battle of Jutland of 1916; they were originally buried here together before being transferred to Gothenburg.

Coming here from Tuvesvik on Orust, a journey of around 30km, the best routing takes you via Ellös and then two free car ferries which cross between Fröjdental and Malö and then again between Ängön and Fruvik. A passenger ferry operates across the mouth of Gullmarsfjorden to nearby Lysekil, a journey of around 12 minutes. Another option is to hire a bike from the tourist office in Lysekil (**w** vastsverige.com/lysekil) and then take the ferry (3 daily late Jul–mid-Aug; 30mins; 75kr) from Lysekil to Grundsund from where you can cycle to Fiskebäckskil – a distance of around 5km. There's good food on offer at the nearby restaurants – Brygghuset (see box opposite for details) and Gullmarsstrand (**w** gullmarsstrand.se; 2-course dinner 425kr) which also has hotel rooms from 2,345kr – see website for details. Alternatively, check out the uniquely decorated rooms at Slipens Hotell & Pensionat (Fiskebäckskilsvägen 28; **w** slipenshotell.se; dbl 1,895kr), for something really quite stylish.

SWEDEN'S ONLY FJORD: GULLMARSFJORDEN

At 25km in length, Gullmarsfjorden, which separates Fiskebäckskil from Lysekil and reaches all the way inland towards Munkedal, is what's known as a threshold fjord: a fjord which is shallower at its mouth than further inland along its course. This difference in depth (20–40m at its mouth and up to 119m elsewhere) creates the ideal conditions for a unique marine environment to develop, and within the fjord there are several protected species of fish. In 2004, even an oceanic whitetip shark (normally found no further north than Portugal) was discovered. A free car ferry operates between Finnsbo and Skår, taking around 10 minutes, vastly reducing journey times and distances to Lysekil. Incidentally, the name *Gullmar* stems from Old Norse and means 'God's sea'.

The shellfish in West Sweden is among the tastiest in the world thanks to the region's cold, clean waters. Visitors can indulge in the region's 'Shellfish Journey' throughout the year, tucking into the many delicacies which are cultivated just offshore, including lobster, mussels, oysters, and langoustines – and learning how to catch and cook them on a unique seafood safari.

Seafood safaris are on offer across Sweden's west coast. Everts Sjöbod (w evertssjobod.se) offers lobster and oyster safaris leaving from their restored 19th-century boathouse in the fishing village of Grebbestad (page 51). Lobster and crayfish safaris are also available through Smögen Fiske & Skärgårdsturer (w fisketur.se), whilst Sörviks Havsservice runs lobster safaris from Marstrand (w fiskahummer.se). Crayfish safaris can be also enjoyed in Fjällbacka with MS *Mira* (w msmira.se). Lysekil Ostron & Musslor (w lysekilsostronomusslor.se/tours) takes visitors on mussel safaris from Lysekil. The boat trip lasts around 2 hours 30 minutes and takes you, first of all, to the local oyster and mussel beds where owner, Adriaan, generally dives to collect the seafood that you subsequently sample for lunch. The boat then heads to a nearby island where *moules marinières* are rustled up over a gas stove – it doesn't get fresher than this. Alternatively, Musselbaren (w musselbaren.se) also runs mussel safaris from Ljungskile.

Seafood safaris operate from April to November and should be booked in advance; full details are available on the relevant websites and waterproof clothing is provided. For more information on seafood safaris in the region, see w vastsverige.com/en/seafood-safaris.

LYSEKIL

Lysekil (roughly pronounced *loo-suh-sheel*) is quite simply the largest place for miles around and, accordingly, is a good place to stock up on supplies and sample some of the cafés and restaurants in town. However, what makes Lysekil really worth a visit is the chance to take a **seafood safari** out to the mussel and oyster beds offshore (see box above) and then sample the seafood yourself. As you entered Lysekil, heading down the gentle hill which leads towards the town centre, you probably spotted the imposing **church** which dominates the entire skyline and is regularly used by seafarers as a guiding landmark. It's built from pink Bohus granite in neo-Gothic style, dates from between 1899 and 1901 and, most significantly, contains a pulpit carved in 1670 in Stralsund, Germany.

HAVETS HUS (w havetshus.se; admission 120kr) Down by the sea at Strandvägen 9, Havets Hus is a fascinating museum of marine life containing around 40 different aquaria full of creatures from the deep. With everything from sharks and rays to starfish and crabs, you'll come face to face with a wide variety of marine fauna which lives in the waters off Lysekil – most excitingly from within the 8m-long underwater tunnel which runs through one of the aquaria. You'll also find information about the marine research which is carried out in Gullmarsfjorden.

STÅNGEHUVUD HEADLAND From Havets Hus it's a 10-minute stroll west out to Lysekil's best beach, **Pinnevik**, next to the football pitch at the junction of Turistgatan and Vikenvägen. From here a walking path continues to the rocky **Stångehuvud**

headland which is composed of pink Bohus granite. Appalled by quarrying activity on the peninsula in the early 1900s, local author, philanthropist and wife of Dr Carl Curman (see below), Calla Curman successively bought bit after bit of the headland to protect the unique character of Stångehuvud. She succeeded and today the headland is a protected nature reserve.

CURMANS VILLOR (℡ 05 23 130 50; **w** curmansvillor.se; contact tourist office for opening times) The ornate, Viking-inspired Curmans Villor, complete with carved dragons and snakes and whose upper storey weirdly juts out above the ground floor, looks like a cross between a Swiss chalet and a Norwegian stave church. It was built in 1880 for Carl Curman, a doctor who liberally prescribed the taking of fresh air and bathing in cold sea water as a cure for all known ills – handy, as he owned the bathhouses his patients were encouraged to pay to use. It was, however, thanks to him that Lysekil developed into Sweden's first health and bathing resort during the latter part of the 19th century. The villas are privately owned but are open to visitors on occasion during the summer and autumn months.

Lysekil's imposing church dominates the skyline (Jonas Ingman)

COLD-WATER BATHHOUSE (**w** lysekilkallbadhus.se) Dating from 1864, Lysekil's *kallbadhus* is open all year round and is free of charge to use. Inside the wooden structure there are gender-segregated sea pools which are used for **nude bathing**. You'll find it to the south of the Curmans Villor and by the marina where there's a jetty which leads to the main entrance.

SMÖGEN AND AROUND

From Lysekil it's an easy drive of around 50km out to one of the west coast's classic destinations: Smögen. This tiny fishing village, linked to the mainland by an arching bridge, has been attracting tourists since the early 1900s when it established itself as a well-to-do bathing resort. Today it's one of the liveliest places on the west coast and positively heaves with visitors during the peak summer season from mid-June to mid-August. Smögen is best known for its 600m-long wooden jetty, known as **Smögenbryggan**. A stroll along its length will take you past any number of chi-chi boutiques selling fashionable clothes, artwork, handicrafts and other knick-knacks, which now occupy the former boathouses and fishing huts. Yachts also tie up here for a day or two and there's often quite a party atmosphere down on the jetty as yachties and tourists fill the plentiful restaurants and cafés which line the waterside.

The 600m-long jetty at Smögen (Åsa Dahlgren)

Smögen is a great place for a **seafood safari** – for details on various tours and companies, see box, page 44. These 'Safaris' offer a chance to put out to sea with a local skipper to fish for seafood before heading back to shore to sample your catch. If you prefer to stay on dry land, there are plenty of hiking tours from Smögen, too: a good option is the trail out to the nature reserve at Ramsvik (for details, see: w vastsverige.com/en/nature-experiences/walking/walking-in-west-sweden).

HÅLLÖ Smögen's best bathing options, all **smooth rocks** rather than sandy strands, are found on the tiny island of Hållö, barely a 10-minute boat ride away from Smögenbryggan. Hållö, which has been declared a nature reserve, is composed of flat granite rocks scraped smooth by the retreating ice during the last Ice Age. The best of all the beaches is the exceptional **Marmorbassängen**, located on the island's western shore, where the water is turquoise blue and exceptionally clear and the surrounding rocks bear a distinct pinky colour. There's a youth hostel and café (w utposthallo.se; dbl room from 600kr) on the island, close to the lighthouse.

NORDENS ARK (w nordensark.se; admission 250kr) Readily accessible via Route 171 between Smögen and Lysekil, Nordens Ark is one of the real highlights of West Sweden. This superbly run **wildlife sanctuary** on the forested shores of the Åby fjord is home to around a hundred endangered species and offers a not-to-be-missed opportunity to get up close to some of the world's rarest animals, birds and amphibians – all of which thrive in the Swedish climate. Providing refuge for snow leopards, Amur tigers, wolves, wolverines and red pandas (to name but a few), this non-profit organisation, founded in 1989, also conducts breeding and research programmes in an effort to save some of the 1.2 million species threatened with extinction; every year 45,000 species disappear from our world. At nearly 400ha, the sanctuary is truly vast, though only a fraction of it is open to the public.

A **walking trail** will lead you around the site and, to see the whole thing at a leisurely pace, you should allow 2–3 hours. Should you want to stay in the area, why not treat yourself at the Vann Spa hotel, 12km to the east at Lingådde in Brastad (☏ 0523/442 00; w vann.se).

Stenugnsbageri Barely a 5-minute drive from Nordens Ark sanctuary along Route 171 towards Smögen will bring you to a great place for a bite to eat:

INGRID BERGMAN AND FJÄLLBACKA

Ingrid Bergman (1915–82) visited Fjällbacka every summer between 1958 and her death in 1982 except one. With her husband, the theatre impresario Lars Schmidt, she lived in a simple house on the long and narrow island of Dannholmen, about 20 minutes by boat northwest of Fjällbacka. During her summer holidays, she often popped into Fjällbacka to go shopping, relishing the relative anonymity the quiet Swedish town offered her, far from the spotlight of Hollywood. She delighted in throwing summer parties on Dannholmen, inviting friends such as Diana Ross and Alfred Hitchcock, and throwing tiny Fjällbacka into quite a spin. It was Bergman's last wish that some of her ashes be scattered in the small bay on the island's northern shore. Today, as you sail out to Väderöarna, you may just catch a glimpse of Dannholmen – keep an eye out for a massive statue of a peace dove which Lars Schmidt had raised on the island in June 1995 in connection with the war in the Balkans.

Lyckans Stenugnsbageri (**w** stenugnsbageri.se). Overlooking a wildflower meadow, this organic café serves up a tempting array of tasty sandwiches and snacks. All the bread here is baked in a birchwood-fired stone oven which makes all the sourdough loaves in particular wonderfully crusty.

FJÄLLBACKA AND AROUND

Located at the foot of an imposing 74m-high granite cliff known as Vetteberget, Fjällbacka is a picture-perfect little village whose houses are painted in fondant shades and decorated with a wealth of intricate gingerbread designs known as *snickarglädje* (carpenter's joy). Indeed, the cliff and its accompanying ravine, **Kungsklyftan**, form the village's main sight; the ravine was named after King Oscar II who visited the town in 1886. At 20m deep and 5m wide, the ravine is dominated by four massive boulders, deposited by the inland ice and now wedged between the rock walls of the gorge. From the top of Vetteberget there are sweeping views of the islands which make up the Fjällbacka archipelago. In the central main square, down at the harbour, you'll find a statue of the Swedish-born Hollywood actress, **Ingrid Bergman** (see box, page 47), who spent many a summer on the island of Dannholmen, just offshore.

VÄDERÖARNA ISLANDS Some 13km offshore and consequently Sweden's most westerly islands, Väderöarna are really something special. Exposed to the elements, this group of 365 wild and barren islands, islets and skerries have one of Sweden's warmest, yet windiest climates – this is a place to experience nature in the raw and witness the mighty power of the sea and the wind. Keep an eye out for seals, too – Sweden's largest seal colony can be found on the rocks around the islands. As you approach by boat from Fjällbacka or Hamburgsund, it's easy to believe that the main island, **Storö**, in the northern section of the Väderöarna chain, is totally void of all vegetation. However, on closer inspection, it's clear that the unusual climatic conditions have given rise to some curiously lush vegetation: the island supports a well-established grove of trees as well as honeysuckle, various grasses and bushes that flourish out of the ever-present wind, hunkered down between the large boulders and rocks which are strewn across the island. Accordingly, the islands were declared a nature reserve in 2012.

The beautiful Väderöarna Islands (Hans Schub)

Värdshuset One of the most agreeable places to stay on the entire Bohuslän coast, Väderöarnas Värdshus (**w** vaderoarna.com) is an extraordinary guesthouse. With just 15 snug little rooms, some with private facilities, this remote island getaway is the ideal place to come to experience peace and quiet and wake up to some stunning sea views – and a hearty breakfast. There's a restaurant here too, and the guesthouse, which is open all year, also boasts a sauna and two hot tubs right by the water's edge. You'll find full details about the ferry journey on the guesthouse website, as well as a number of package deals.

Walks around Storö From the guesthouse, where the boat from Fjällbacka puts in, a **walking trail** loops north around most of Storö – it's takes about 40 minutes or so to complete. The trail is marked by wooden stakes hammered into the rock and includes several sections of duckboarding and steps to negotiate the more tricky sections of the island terrain. Having climbed up to **Husestadsberget**, one of the highest points on the island, the trail cuts down to an elongated lake, **Näckhöljen**, which comes as quite a surprise – it's hard to believe that the island can conceal such a relatively sizeable body of water from virtually every angle. From the lake, the trail then continues south, returning to the guesthouse via the **Östra Hamnen harbour**. If you walk the trail in the evening, keep an eye out for the island's toads which emerge at this time of day. They thrive here as the island has no grass snakes (nor ticks for that matter). Incidentally, a few years ago, there was even a vixen and her cub on the island – it's thought she reached Väderöarna by walking and floating on the sea ice during the winter.

Pilot's lookout (Follow the signs marked 'Utkik'; ⊕ when the flag is flying) From the guesthouse, it's an easy climb up a set of steps to the pilot's lookout **station**, located at the southern end of Storö. The first lookout was established in 1754 to help ships negotiate the treacherous array of islands and skerries which mark the sea approach to Fjällbacka. Although operations ceased between 1966 and 1967, the tower has been recently renovated and during the summer months is often open for viewing. A near-vertical staircase leads up to the lookout point itself, which affords sterling views of the Fjällbacka archipelago. Incidentally, the wind speed up here is recorded by an anemometer in the guesthouse reception.

Bronze Age rock carvings beside the Vitlycke Museum (Vitlycke Museum)

TANUM ROCK CARVINGS Another must-see lies within easy striking distance of Fjällbacka: the greatest concentration of **Bronze Age rock carvings** anywhere in Scandinavia, many over 3,000 years old, and a UNESCO World Heritage Site. The area surrounding the town of **Tanumshede**, about 17km north of Fjällbacka, boasts no fewer than 1,500 of them, grouped into 12 main sites, and constitutes an outstanding example of European Bronze Age art. During the Bronze Age (1700–500BC), Tanumshede was coastal as the sea level was around 15m higher than it is today. Travelling by boat, people frequented this area and began scratching the images into the ice-smoothed rock in the early part of the Bronze Age, returning over the following centuries to carve yet more figures. It's clear that the site played an important role in the life of the Bronze Age people who lived here, though whether it bore a religious significance or a purely social one remains uncertain. However the carvings are interpreted, the range of motifs offers a remarkable insight into Bronze Age life: people, weapons, wild animals and boats are all portrayed, though never their dwellings, fields or pigs.

Carving sites The greatest concentration of carvings is found around the tiny village of **Vitlycke**, a couple of kilometres south of Tanumshede, and it's here that you will find the four main viewing sites: Vitlycke, Aspeberget, Litsleby and Fossum. The rock panel at Vitlycke, located beside the museum (**w** vitlyckemuseum.se; free entry), contains around 100 large carvings, predominantly of boats and people. **Aspeberget**, 700m south of the museum, portrays bulls, warriors and ships. The **Litsleby** panel, 2km south of the museum, is dominated by a huge warrior, 2.3m tall, the so-called 'spear god', while **Fossum**, around 3km from the museum, contains a wide mix of carvings – people, ships, the soles of human feet and animals. You are not allowed to walk on the rock panels themselves, but you are free to discover the rock carvings, or, alternatively, you can take the once-daily guided tour; see the website for details.

Bridal couple carving One frequently recurring image is that of a man with an erect penis – doubtless a sign of fertility – a theme that is repeated in the best known of all the carvings, the '**bridal couple**', which appears on the rock panel at Vitlycke itself. It seems to depict a fornicating couple standing upright and it's been suggested that the carving may refer to either a holy wedding or an act of intercourse between the god of fertility and a woman with the aim of securing fertility for both man and animals. It's thought the ritual was carried out in the spring with a priest or other cult figure playing the role of a god.

Museum and farm For more background on the Bronze Age itself, have a look inside the museum (see details on page 50), which has several thoughtful **exhibitions** about the period and the rock carvings themselves; there's also a **café** and a **shop** here. Behind the museum, a reconstruction of a Bronze Age farm contains two **longhouses** which were typical dwellings and a fenced **garden** where herbs and plants used during the Bronze Age are cultivated. During the summer months there are also activities such as the making of bronze items, pottery and food in which visitors can participate.

GREBBESTAD Barely 8km southwest of Vitlycke, back on the coast, Grebbestad is oyster country par excellence: 90% of all of Sweden's **oysters** come from here. Thanks to Grebbestad's cool, clear waters, it's said that the oysters found here are the best in the world. Whether or not that's true, there's no better place to sample oysters in this neck of the woods than at **Everts Sjöbod** (Grönemadsvägen 61, Grönmad; w evertssjobod.se; fishing & lesson 790kr), located a couple of kilometres outside of Grebbestad; to get here, turn right just before the church when entering Grebbestad from the north and then left into Grönemadsvägen at the sign for Grönemad. Here you fish for your own oysters by using a large fishing net before taking them inside for a lesson on how to deftly open them – quite a skill. Alternatively, there's the option of taking a boat tour (approx 2hrs 30mins) out to the oyster beds and sampling oysters on board – there's a good chance of seeing seals on the trip, too. There's full information online, plus details of the overnight accommodation also on offer. Everts Sjöbod is open all year but advance booking is always required. Incidentally, Grebbestad is also ideally situated for a spot of sea kayaking – the waters hereabouts are protected from swells and large waves by the dozens of islands offshore. Just 3km south of Grebbestad, **Tanumstrand** (w tanumstrand.se) offers more waterside accommodation in the form of cosy cottages and regular hotel rooms.

There's seemingly no end to the types of safari you can do in West Sweden: why not try a seaweed safari with Catxalot (w catxalot.se) in nearby Grönemad who will teach you which type of seaweed is good to eat, among other things!

STRÖMSTAD

About 30km north of Tanumshede, the once fashionable 18th-century spa resort, **Strömstad**, has an air of faded grandeur. Everywhere of interest is easily accessible from its train station or the ferry port opposite – Strömstad is linked by Color Line boats to Sandefjord in Norway. If you're heading for Kosteröarna, you're bound to pass through the town – if you find yourself with a couple of hours to kill before jumping on the catamaran over to the islands, have a look around and you'll find several worthwhile diversions.

Although you wouldn't guess it from its run-of-the-mill exterior, the inside of Strömstad's **church**, a few minutes' walk from the train station, has an eclectic mix of unusual decorative features, including busy frescoes, model ships hanging from the roof and gilt chandeliers. Close by, the **Konsthallen Lokstallet** (Uddevallavägen 1; w konsthallenlokstallet.se) arts venue is worth a quick look. Housed in the town's former railway sheds, the gallery aims to showcase contemporary art and handicrafts.

Strömstad's most bizarre building, which overlooks the whole town, is the massive, copper-roofed **Stadshus**, the product of a millionaire recluse whose architectural meddling is second only to former Romanian dictator Nicolae Ceauşescu. Born to a local jeweller in 1851, the marvellously named Adolf Fritiof

The rugged Kosteröarna are ideal for trekking (Göran Assner)

Cavalli-Holmgren soon became a financial whizz-kid and one of Sweden's richest men. When he heard Strömstad was crying out for a town hall he offered to finance it on two conditions: it had to be built on the spot his parents had lived and he had to have complete control over its design. By the time of its completion in 1917, he was no longer on speaking terms with the city's politicians and never returned to see the structure, which even had a penthouse suite for his private use. Much later, in 1951, it was discovered that his obsessive devotion to his parents had led him to design the entire building around the dates of their birthdays: 27 January and 14 May and their wedding day, 7 March. The dimensions of the 100-plus rooms were calculated using combinations of the numbers in the dates, as were the sizes of every window, every flight of stairs and every cluster of lamps. Furthermore, he only ever responded or held meetings with town officials on these dates.

Strömstad has two swanky hotels: the centrally located **Laholmen** (w laholmen.se), perched on a little hill above the marina, and **Strömstad Spa** (w stromstadspa.se), an ultra-modern spa complex, a 10-minute walk from the town centre at Kebalvägen 229. In Strömstad, why not treat yourself to some delicious fresh fish: you'll find a great selection at **Rökeriet i Strömstad** (w stromstad.com/restauranger/rokeriet), opposite the train station at Torskholmen.

KOSTERHAVET NATIONAL PARK

The Kosteröarna islands are separated from the mainland by the deep trench of **Kosterfjorden** which reaches an astonishing depth of 247m. The trench continues all the way out to the North Atlantic continental shelf allowing cold, salty oceanic water to flow into the fjord – this makes it possible for many deep-sea animals to live so close to the coast. The waters around the islands, known as **Kosterhavet**, have been declared a **marine national park** and are home to around 12,000 species both above and below the surface as well as Sweden's largest seal colony. There's a free exhibition about the marine park inside the **Visitor Centre** (free entry) at the ferry jetty in Ekenäs on Sydkoster; more information can also be found at w kosterhavet.se.

SALTÖ NATURE RESERVE Roughly 12km southwest of Strömstad and barely 3km across Kosterfjorden from the southeastern tip of Sydkoster, the island of Saltö is one of the most visited **nature reserves** in the whole of Bohuslän – and with good reason. People come here to enjoy the superb sandy beaches, stroll through the coastal pine forest (which is only found in this part of the province) and to fish from the island's western coast. There's even an underwater **snorkel trail** marked with a blue line at a depth of around 1–1.5m which leads to eight information boards – also under the water – and the beginning and end of the trail are marked by buoys. The best **beaches** are found on the southern shore – from the (pay) car park by the main road, simply follow either of the two footpaths for around 1km or so through the forest – both lead to the beaches. One beach is found on the south coast while the other is on the east coast and is also the location of the snorkel trail.

Kattholmen nudist beach Kattholmen is a tiny rocky island which lies off the southeastern shore of Saltö. It's a favourite destination for sunbathing 'in the altogether' as there's a wonderfully relaxed nudist beach located on the western side of the islet. To reach Kattholmen, first park at the car park on Saltö, then follow the footpath which leads off to the right by the information board; look out for the word 'Nakenbad' (nudist beach) written on the rocks. Then, at the shore, wade across to Kattholmen through the shallow water for about 20m.

KOSTERÖARNA

Sweden's westernmost inhabited islands, Kosteröarna, or the Koster islands, 10km off Strömstad, are a real highlight of any trip along the Bohuslän coast. Not only do the islands enjoy more hours of sunshine than virtually anywhere else in the country but they are ideally suited to leisurely exploration by bike or on foot – a haven of peace and quiet, Kosteröarna are generally car-free. Rural **Sydkoster** boasts one of the best and biggest sandy beaches on the entire west coast (see below), and rugged **Nordkoster** has dramatic scenery aplenty (page 55).

SYDKOSTER Of the two Kosters, most people make a beeline for Sydkoster – the larger and more leafy of the two islands. The two main settlements, Ekenäs and Kyrkosund, neither little more than a village, both lie on the east coast separated by a long and totally unspoilt stretch of **sandy beach** backed by pine forest,

Bohuslän Coast   KOSTERÖARNA

3

The Kosterhavet marine national park is home to Sweden's largest seal colony (Mikael Almse)

Kilesand – one of Sydkoster's real gems. You can reach Kilesand easily from Ekenäs by following the coastal **footpath** south for a kilometre or two; **bike rental** is available at the ferry jetty (**w** kostercykeln.com). Indeed, Sydkoster is made for cycling in the sun, along easy paths through wild flower meadows; once in a while you can stop for refreshments at the smattering of small cafés and ice-cream parlours or better still at **Kosters Trädgårdar** (**w** kosterstradgardar.se; see box, page 42, for details), a glorious restaurant and café set in a delightful garden on the lane between the island church and Långegärde. Eighty per cent of the organic produce served is grown on site and there are even musical performances during the summer months. For details, see the restaurant website.

If you visit both of the Koster islands, you'll soon realise that Sydkoster is altogether more pastoral and wooded than its more barren neighbour to the north. Wild roses and angelica grow readily on the shoreline here and a little inland there are dense groves of birch and hazel. A pleasant **cycle ride** and **walk** will take you through some of the island's pretty woodland starting from just south of the church and leading west out to **Långevik bay** – you have to leave your bike for the last stretch as the path goes through a nature reserve. Here, on the west coast, there are uninterrupted views of the dozens of islands and skerries which lie off Sydkoster's southwestern coast. Långevik is also a good place to **snorkel** – just to the left of the beach there are any number of giant oysters, hermit crabs and species of flat fish. Sydkoster is also an easy place to arrange either a lobster or seal safari – contact Selin Charter for more details (**w** selincharter.se).

Back in Ekenäs, where the ferry docks from Strömstad, you'll find the best place to stay on the island: **Hotel Ekenäs Koster** (**w** hotelkoster.se). The hotel sits

Ursholmen Island in the Kosterhavet marine national park (Mikael Almse)

on a rocky bluff offering superb sea views from both its rooms and the outdoor deck, where you can savour some of the most succulent seafood you'll ever taste while breathing in the fresh sea air perfumed with the scent of honeysuckle, lady's bedstraw and tangy seaweed. Alternatively, **Kostergården** (w kostergarden. com) at Kyrkosundsvägen 1, near the ferry jetty at Kilesand, offers comfortable accommodation in either cabins or apartments, all overlooking the sea.

NORDKOSTER Reached by cable ferry from Långegärde in the northwestern corner of Sydkoster, Nordkoster, half the size of its southern neighbour, is an altogether more craggy and angular sort of place. Dominated by the hill, **Högen** (59m), in the middle of the island, the two **lighthouses** you can see here operated until 1891. Elsewhere, Nordkoster is composed of rocky outcrops, between which areas of heather and various other shrubs and bushes flourish protected from the wind. Since bikes are not allowed on Nordkoster, the only way to explore is on foot. A 3.5km **walking path** leads around the island from the foot of Högen – one of the island's best **sandy beaches** is found in the far northeast, sheltered by the islet, **Korsholmen**, just offshore. Returning west via **Pumpedalen** and its unusual rock features, you'll come to the second of Nordkoster's beaches, **Basteviken**, in the southwestern corner of the island. There are several places to stay on the island, including a campsite, and there's also a grocery store and a restaurant. During the summer season you can easily travel between the two islands on the cable ferry that runs between Långegärde (Sydkoster) and Västra Bryggan (Nordkoster). During the rest of the year you should ask locally about the best way to cross.

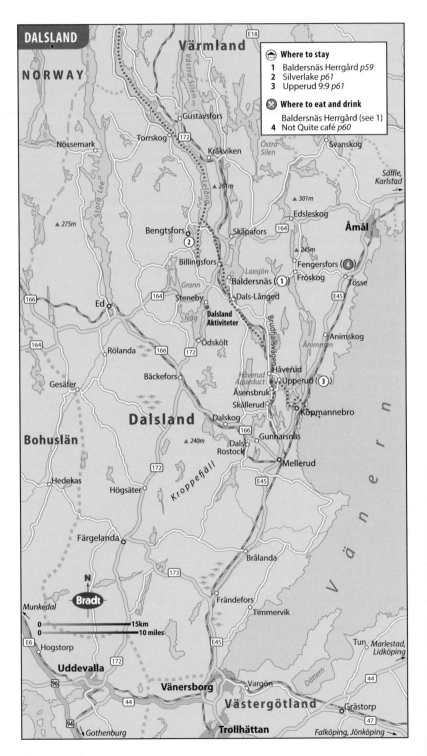

DALSLAND

Värmland

NORWAY

🛏 **Where to stay**
1 Baldersnäs Herrgård *p59*
2 Silverlake *p61*
3 Upperud 9:9 *p61*

❌ **Where to eat and drink**
   Baldersnäs Herrgård (see 1)
4 Not Quite café *p60*

Gustavsfors

Torrskog [172]
Nössemark   Kråkviken   *Östra*   Svanskog
                                      Silen
                                                        Säffle,
                                                        Karlstad
                          ▲261m
                                          ▲301m
▲275m   Edsleskog
          Bengtsfors   Skåpafors [164]   **Åmål**
              ②
                                      ▲245m
            Billingsfors   *Laxsjön*   Fengersfors ④
                          Grann   Baldersnäs ①   Fröskog   Tösse
[166]   Ed   [164] Steneby   Dals-Långed   [E45]
                          Ivåg **Dalsland**
                                  Aktiviteter   Animskog
[164]   Ödskölt   *Animmen*
          Rölanda [166] [172]
                                      Håverud Håverud
    Gesäter   Bäckefors   *Aqueduct* ⌂Upperud ③
                              Åsensbruk
                              Skållerud
                                  Dalskog   ⌂Köpmannebro
              Dalsland   Dalskog
Bohuslän   ▲240m   Dals   Gunnarsnäs
                              Rostock
       Hedekas   ⌂Mellerud
              Högsäter   *Kroppefjäll* [E45]

          Färgelanda
                                  Brålanda

              N   [173]
     Munkedal **Bradt**   Frändefors
                                      Timmervik
       0 ━━━━━━━ 15km
       0 ━━━━━━ 10 miles
[E6] Hogstorp   [E45]   Tun *Marlestad,*
                                                Lidköping
    Uddevalla [172]
[96]   **Vänersborg** Vargön   [44]
       [44]   **Västergötland** ⌂Grästorp
[94]   [47]
    Gothenburg   **Trollhättan** *Falköping, Jönköping* →

56

4

Dalsland

Sandwiched between Bohuslän to the west and Lake Vänern to the east, the province of Dalsland is West Sweden at its most rural. Sparsely populated, Dalsland is truly a land of lakes and forests; there are few towns here and the only settlement of any size, uneventful Åmål (pronounced *oh-mole*), located in the far northeast of the region, sees few visitors. But nobody comes to Dalsland for its towns – instead the area is known for its great range of **outdoor activities** which make full use of the unspoilt nature which abounds here: fishing, kayaking, horseriding, hiking, even pedalling a railbike along disused railway tracks are all popular. Dalsland is also the location for one of the region's latest and most unusual attractions: a stay in a **cabin made of glass**, rather than wood, allowing you to completely surround yourself by the sights and sounds of Swedish nature (see box, page 59). Indeed, the cuisine here takes its cue from the great outdoors, too: game, freshwater fish, berries and mushrooms all feature prominently on the menu. The place to aim for is **Dals-Långed**, a small village roughly in the centre of the province, from where you're within easy reach of the main attractions – and also one of the most idyllic places to stay (see Baldersnäs Herrgård, page 59). If, however, you're looking for something less energetic, head for **Bengtsfors**, a modest little place in the north of Dalsland, from where you can take a boat trip along the graceful Dalsland Canal (see box, page 62), with its 30-odd locks, down to Håverud where you'll find Sweden's one-and-only aqueduct.

Truly a land of lakes and forests, Dalsland is a haven for outdoor enthusiasts (Roger Borgelid)

GETTING AROUND DALSLAND

Although a car is always going to be the best way to get around Dalsland, with perseverance you can also discover large parts of the province by public transport. **Trains** between Gothenburg and Karlstad (in neighbouring Värmland) connect a number of towns in the east of the province along the shores of Lake Vänern, while services from Gothenburg to Oslo run via western Dalsland. Between late June and late August **private trains** also operate between Bengtsfors and Mellerud via Dals-Långed; see **w** dvvj.se for more details. **Buses** help to fill in the gaps and offer the only way of getting around the north of the province. Full details are available at **w** vasttrafik.se.

HIKING THE PILGRIMS' TRAIL

Spanning over 100km of tremendously varied terrain, the **Pilgrims' Trail** stretches from Vänersborg in the south of Dalsland to Åmål in the north. The name stems from the time when the path was walked by pilgrims on their way to holy Nidaros (present-day Trondheim) in Norway, which was northern Europe's most important pilgrimage site during the Middle Ages. Between Vänersborg and Upperud the trail is suitable for everyone as it follows quiet country roads and footpaths, passing several medieval churches along the way. North of Upperud it traverses more challenging landscapes, characterised by steep gradients and ravines, as well as areas of pristine wilderness. It's an ideal way to get close to nature – there are several places to break the journey overnight and public transport options, too. Upperud 9:9, for example, offers a special three-night Pilgrims' Trail package, including accommodation, transport and food. Local tourist offices have plenty more information, or see **w** vastsverige.com/en/nature-experiences/walking/pilgrimsleden-in-dalsland.

The varied terrain of the Pilgrims' Trail offers opportunities for hikers of all abilities (Henrik Trygg)

THE GLASS CABINS OF DALSLAND

How do you fancy an overnight stay deep in the heart of the forest, surrounded by Swedish nature up close? Dalsland now has a network of what are called **72-hour cabins**, each in effect **a glass-walled cottage**, dotted around the province in prime remote locations, allowing you to experience nature at first hand. Tests have shown that a stay of anything up to three nights in the glass cabins radically reduces stress and anxiety levels and leads to a drop in blood pressure and an increased sense of well-being. By day, there are plenty of activities on hand like canoeing, fishing, hiking or swimming, while by night you can drift off to sleep observing the stars through your glass roof. Find your glass cabin and more information at **w** 72hcabin.com.

Dalsland has a network of '72-hour cabins' set in stunning remote locations, where you can stay and experience nature first-hand (Jonas Ingman)

4

DALS-LÅNGED AND AROUND

Blink and you'll miss Dals-Långed, a tiny village, home to around 1,500 people on the shores of Lake Laxsjön. Although the settlement is not a destination in itself, it makes a good place to aim for as it's ideally located to reach a number of surrounding attractions. Close by, there's an elegant manor house, Baldernäs Herrgård which makes a superb place to stay or have dinner, and the province's leading activities centre, **Dalslands Aktiviteter**, is also with easy reach. Around 20km north of Dals-Långed, Bengtsfors is the main town in these parts. It's from here that boats ply the serene waters of the Dalsland Canal on their way south to Håverud. Nearby Upperud makes a great place to spend the night if you've arrived by boat and don't want to return immediately to Bengtsfors.

BALDERSNÄS HERRGÅRD Located just 6km north of Dals-Långed, within a nature reserve jutting out into Lake Laxsjön, **Baldersnäs Herrgård** (**w** baldersnas.eu; dbl rooms from 895kr) is a handsome, lakeside manor house that was built between 1910 and 1912. This classically symmetrical three-storey stone mansion

EXPLORING DALSLAND'S DISUSED RAILWAYS

One of the most fun – and unusual – things to do in Dalsland is to pedal a specially constructed **railbike** along one of the province's disused railway lines, closed to passenger services since 1985. The railbikes (*dressin* in Swedish) ride along the rails like a conventional train carriage but are driven by pedal power – you sit on a bike saddle and simply pedal the railbike down the track. You can hire the railbikes for anything from an hour or two to several days, camping along the way; the disused railway line stretches for 52km from **Bengtsfors** across the provincial border to Årjäng in Värmland; full details are available at w dvvj.se and you can start your journey from either end.

with two side pavilions is surrounded by well-tended parkland which slopes gently down to the shores of the lake. The building has been restored to how it looked during the 1940s and makes a delightful place to stay – either in the main building itself (where some rooms contain the original tiled fireplaces) or in one of the two modern wings down by the lake. Alternatively, the manor house also rents out glass cabins (see box, page 59). The restaurant here prides itself on serving locally sourced, often organic, produce. From mid-June to late August, it's possible to catch the Dalsland **canal boats** at Baldersnäs – though advance booking is required for these departures (see box, page 62 for contact details for the boat operators).

FENGERSFORS In the opposite direction from Dals-Långed, around 18km to the northeast, little-known **Fengersfors** is worth seeking out for its unusual displays of modern art. Here, in a former paper mill, which closed in the late 70s, a group of local artists have opened an innovative arts complex. **Not Quite** (Fabriksvägen 2; w notquite.se), as the venture is known, uses rough-and-ready, post-industrial buildings to maximum effect by exhibiting paintings, sculptures and other artwork in among the rusting machinery from the old paper-making days. In addition to the art displays, music and opera performances are also held here, plus there's a café serving organically produced lunches and sandwiches, a gift shop and a gallery. Full details of all exhibitions and events can be found on the website.

DALSLANDS AKTIVITETER (Dalsland Activities; w dalslandsaktiviteter.com) Around 10km west of Dals-Långed, Dalslands Aktiviteter is *the* place to make for if you're looking to get out into the wilds and experience first-hand what Dalsland is really all about. Established in 1993, the activities centre is open all year round and offers a whole host of **outdoor pursuits** – full details are available online. A special favourite is the zip line, which, at 40m above the ground and 600m long, is the longest in the country. However, there's also abseiling, rock climbing and even a giant swing should you want even more excitement. Alternatively, the centre also offers fishing, horseriding and kayaking – or why not try archery, gold-panning or mountain biking? You name it, it's available, including a stay in a glass cabin (see box, page 59). There's also an **elk park** where you can get up close to the king of the forest. Overnight accommodation is also available (see website for details).

SILVERLAKE CANOEING (w silverlake.se) Dalsland has more lakes per square kilometre than any other region of Sweden – over a thousand at the last count. Getting out on to the water is one of the most enjoyable things to do in the province and the best place for it lies just 30km north of Dals-Långed at **Kråkviken**. Here, in the very north of the province at Silverlake Canoeing, you can hire kayaks and canoes for anything from one day to one week; suggested itineraries can be viewed on the website. It's also possible to combine a kayak/canoe trip with railbiking on the disused railway line between Årjäng and Bengtsfors or with hiking through some of the unspoilt forests in the area. Silverlake also has overnight accommodation available (see website for details).

HÅVERUD AND UPPERUD Though **Håverud** is pleasant enough as the destination for a trip on the Dalsland Canal, other than its aqueduct and modest Kanalmuseum at Museivägen 3 (w kanalmuseet.se; admission 40kr), which recounts the history of the canal and the lives of some of the families who have lived along its course over the generations, there's little else to see in the village itself. Instead, take a trip to nearby **Upperud**, just over 2km to the southeast along Upperudsvägen: its easily walkable if you don't have transport. Housed in a former grain silo from the late 1800s, you'll find one of the best overnight accommodation options for miles: Upperud 9:9 (w upperud.se). There are five stylishly appointed self-catering apartments here (from 1,500kr), right by the lakeside, and all feature the roughly

Exploring the Dalsland Canal by canoe (Roger Borgelid)

THE DALSLAND CANAL

The Dalsland Canal (**w** dalslandskanal.se) runs for 250km between Köpmannebro on Lake Vänern and southwestern Värmland, flowing through a fault in the bedrock. Opened in 1868 to transport timber and iron ore between Värmland's forests and Lake Vänern, only 10km had to be dug, however, as the canal actually makes use of an interconnected network of lakes and waterways over its course. At the canal's southern end, in **Håverud**, the canal passes through an **aqueduct** since the soft bedrock hereabouts made it impossible to build a lock. Between mid-June and late August, two passenger boats, the over 120-year-old MS *Storholmen* (**w** storholmen.com) and MS *Dalslandia* (**w** dalslandia.com) operate between Håverud and Bengtsfors, a journey of around 4 hours 30 minutes, passing through the aqueduct, 16 locks and some exceptionally beautiful countryside; food and drink is available on both boats. Of the two boats, MS *Storholmen* is much the more characterful and a tasty lunch of smoked salmon from Håverud is also served onboard, accompanied by dill potatoes and salad (150kr). A great combination is to take the boat in one direction, say from Bengtsfors to Håverud, and then to return to Bengtsfors by train (total journey time 6hrs); a return ticket for this costs 410kr and full timetable details are available on the MS *Storholmen* website (see above). An annual canoe marathon is also held on the canal and adjoining lakes during the second week of August and makes quite a spectacle as hundreds of people tackle the 55km-long course.

Relax and enjoy the view on the Dalsland Canal (Gaby Karlsson Hain)

hewn planks of the original wooden walls. Be sure to clamber up the 20m-high tower alongside for fabulous views out over the surrounding lake system.

From Håverud one of the most enjoyable road trips in West Sweden unfolds – it may be only 17km back to Bengtsfors, but the **switchback drive** north along Brudfjällsvägen is spectacular. The road twists and turns its entire length, crossing the single-track railway line between the two points twice, and plunging in and out of deep forest all the way. Scudding over rocky outcrops, winding round the tightest of bends and meandering through the hilly post-glacial landscape, this is a glorious way to return to Dals-Långed and Bengtsfors.

5

The Göta Canal and Around

Stretching all the way from Gothenburg to Stockholm, the Göta Canal is one of Sweden's historic landmarks. Sixty thousand workers toiled for 22 years to build it, and today, two hundred years or so after its construction, it remains one of the defining features of West Sweden. The most beguiling stretch lies between the great lakes of Vänern and Vättern in the province of **Västergötland** – a leisurely boat trip or cycle ride between **Sjötorp** and **Töreboda** is a great way to see the canal and the surrounding countryside. For an overnight stop, look no further than the converted mill at **Norrqvarn**, right alongside the canal, where there's an accomplished restaurant, too. At **Karlsborg**, on the western shores of Lake Vättern, you can get to grips with Swedish military history and explore the impressive fortress which was designed to protect Sweden from a possible military invasion during the 19th century. West Sweden's rich industrial heritage is on display in nearby **Forsvik** where you can visit a converted foundry and paper mill. Nature lovers are well served, too: **Tiveden National Park**, north of the canal, boasts a protected area of virgin forest, one of the few in the entire region, and a network of hiking trails provides ready access on foot to some of the giant boulders and deep ravines for which the park is also justifiably known.

SJÖTORP TO TÖREBODA

There are three main ways to explore the Göta Canal between Sjötorp and Töreboda, a distance of around 19km. Arguably, the best is to hop onboard **MS *Bellevue*** (w gotakanal.se) as she makes her way through the 16 locks (they give the canal a height difference of 40m) which span this section of the canal. Lunch is available on board and the whole journey takes 5 hours. Another option is to hire a **bike**

THE GÖTA CANAL

The Göta Canal (w gotakanal.se), completed in 1832, forms the backbone of the 600km waterway which links Gothenburg on the North Sea with Stockholm on the Baltic Sea. Strictly speaking, the Göta Canal is not one but three canals which, linked together by various lakes and the Trollhätte Canal, complete the coast-to-coast route. With no fewer than 58 locks, the canal is still used to transport cargo but tourist and leisure traffic far outnumber all other usage. Passenger boats ply all or parts of the canal and make a graceful way of seeing the rolling landscapes around the canal: **Strömma** (w gotakanal.se) operates between Gothenburg and Stockholm while **MS *Bellevue*** (w gotakanal.se) makes short hops between Sjötorp and Töreboda.

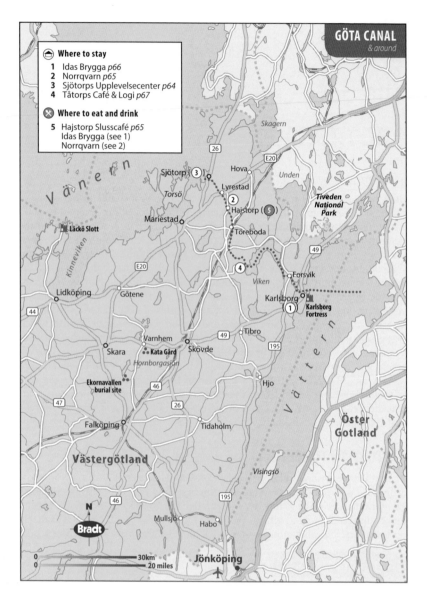

Where to stay
1 Idas Brygga *p66*
2 Norrqvarn *p65*
3 Sjötorps Upplevelsecenter *p64*
4 Tåtorps Café & Logi *p67*

Where to eat and drink
5 Hajstorp Slusscafé *p65*
   Idas Brygga (see 1)
   Norrqvarn (see 2)

and cycle parallel to the bank along a network of well-maintained routes – cycling here is easy since the terrain is flat, with just short inclines as you pass a lock. Bike rental is readily available in Sjötorp from Sjötorps Upplevelsecenter (w cykelsemester.se), where you can hire bikes for anything from a few hours to four days, either with or without accommodation options; full details and information about their youth hostel rooms are online. Further rent-a-bike outlets are to be found in Töreboda, plus at Norrqvarn hotel (see opposite). However, if you consider yourself more paddler than pedaller, why not hire a **canoe** and experience the canal at water level? For all bike and canoe hire details, see w gotakanal.se.

On the way to Töreboda, be sure to stop at Hajstorp, 15km southeast of Sjötorp, where there's a great café, Hajstorp Slusscafé (w hajstorp.com), located in the former lock-keeper's cottage. Next door, you'll find youth hostel accommodation, a small museum with black-and-white photos and old farm implements from the early 1900s.

NORRQVARN (w norrqvarn.se; dbl rooms from 1,190kr) Overlooking the canal just 9km east of Sjötorp, Norrqvarn is a delightful hotel and renowned restaurant serving locally sourced, organic produce, housed in a converted mill just east of Lyrestad (which is easily accessible via the E20 motorway). For a quirky night's stay, why not choose a room inside either a giant tree stump or a red-and-white spotted toadstool – these unusual purpose-built wooden structures are great for children and make a fun overnight stop. The hotel has bikes for hire and it's also possible to go fishing for crayfish in season. It makes a good base to explore the canal as it's halfway between Sjötorp and Töreboda.

KARLSBORG AND AROUND

Despite the great plans devised for the **fortress** of **Karlsborg**, 42km southeast of Töreboda on the western shores of Lake Vättern (Europe's sixth largest), it has survived the years as one of Sweden's greatest follies. By the early 19th century, Sweden had lost Finland to Russia – after 600 years of control – and had become jumpy about its own security. In 1818, with the Russian fleet stationed on the Finnish Åland islands and within easy striking distance of Stockholm, statesman and naval officer Count Baltzar von Platen persuaded parliament to construct an island fortress at Karlsborg. It was to be capable of sustaining an entire town and protecting the royal family and the treasury – the idea being that enemy forces should be lured into the country and then destroyed on Swedish territory. With the town pinched between lakes Vättern and Bottensjön, the Göta Canal – also the

The Norrqvarn hotel is housed in a converted mill on the Göta Canal (Norrqvarn)

brainchild of von Platen and already under construction – was to provide access. Yet, while the Count had the canal finished by 1832, the fortress was so ambitious a project that it took 90 years to complete and the walls were lamentedly declared incapable of withstanding attack from new weaponry innovations.

Today, visitors are free to amble around the complex, which is as big as a small town, but arguably the best option is to take a guided tour. If you have children in tow, opt for the animated hunt for the hidden gold reserves. Details are at **w**.vastsverige.com/en/karlsborg.

For somewhere different to stay in Karlsborg, try the waterside Idas Brygga (**w** idasbrygga.se), right beside the jetty where yachts and boats tackling the canal and lake tie up for the night.

FORSVIK (**w** forsviksbruk.se) As far back as the early 14th century, Karlsborg maintained an important monastic flour mill, 8km to the northwest, at the village of Forsvik, where a monastery was founded by Sweden's first female saint, Birgitta. The height differential between nearby lakes meant that energy could be extracted, first by means of waterwheels and later with turbines, which allowed a sizeable industry to emerge, making all manner of metal and wood products. During the Reformation, the Crown confiscated Forsvik from the monastery. However, the building of the Göta Canal gave the place new life: it once again became a busy industrial centre, with a paper mill operating until the 1940s and a foundry until the Swedish shipyard crises of the 1970s. Today, the area makes for an engaging excursion: the mill has been restored to its 1940s' condition and a number of exhibitions relate the area's industrial heritage.

TÅTORP A pastoral gem of a place, it's hard to beat the accommodation on offer at nearby Tåtorp, around 35km to the west of Forsvik. Here, **Tåtorps Café & Logi** (**w** tatorp.se) has used timber and any number of recycled products to create a haven of peace and tranquillity beside the Göta Canal. Surrounded by apple trees and blackcurrant bushes, the original timber structure, painted in a rich yellow ochre, is the centre of the STF-affiliated youth hostel, while next door a newer building stands amid a grove of birch trees. Tåtorp hires out kayaks, boats and bikes, too.

TIVEDEN NATIONAL PARK (**w** tiveden.se) Located 25km northeast of Karlsborg, Tiveden National Park is part of a much larger expanse of wild forest and rugged terrain which spans the provincial border between Västergötland and neighbouring Närke; the best approach is from the south along Route 49 between Karlsborg and Askersund. One of southern Sweden's few remaining areas of virgin forest, the park has never been inhabited, and today it offers the visitor a chance to explore an environment close to that of a primeval forest, complete with giant boulders and deep rift valleys. With no human intervention, dead trees are left to decay, providing an important habitat for many rare birds and animals. A number of marked hiking trails (covering 25km in total) criss-cross Tiveden's 20km² (the park was extended in early 2017); the most popular trail is the Stenkälle loop (2km), which begins and ends at the park's main entrance, providing access to some of the park's massive boulders and, by climbing a set of steps, you'll have views of Lake Vättern. There's also access from the trail to the swimming beach, Vitsand.

Drift down the Göta Canal on the elegant old ship Juno (Åsa Dahlgren)

6
Västergötland

The undulating farmland south of Lake Vänern and west of Lake Vättern is known as **Västergötland**, an often-overlooked, essentially rural part of West Sweden. Covering a vast area of nearly 17,000km², the province is roughly the same size as Wales, with few large towns or cities. It's at its most appealing in lakeside **Lidköping**, where the nearby hilly plateau of **Kinnekulle** affords spectacular views over the sweeping expanses of Lake Vänern. Fans of Baroque splendour will be enchanted by **Läckö Slott**, a 17th-century castle, just to the north of the town. Moving to the southeast, **Varnhem** with its magnificent abbey, resting place of one of Sweden's greatest statesmen, Birger Jarl, along with the adjacent Viking-age finds at Kata Gård, should not be missed under any circumstances. From here, there's easy access to the remarkable prehistoric burial ground, **Ekornavallen**, with remains dating from the Stone Age to late Iron Age. Close by, the ornithologist's dream, **Hornborgasjön** (Lake Hornborga) attracts up to 18,000 cranes every spring which come here to pair – dancing all day long in the process and making quite an extraordinary sight. Västergötland's main city outside Gothenburg is **Borås**, a bright and breezy place, which attempts to charm visitors through its rich industrial heritage, though, arguably, charming **Alingsås** is a better bet: there are more cafés here than you can shake a teaspoon at and the town makes a perfect place for a *fika*, the quintessential Swedish pastime of drinking coffee and savouring cinnamon buns and princess cake.

One of West Sweden's real historical gems, medieval castle **Torpa Stenhus**, lies close by to the southeast and should be on everyone's list of must-sees. Pretty, little **Ulricehamn** offers lakeside tranquility and hiking and skiing opportunities, barely a few kilometres away. Another of the region's **cross-country skiing** destinations, though, is modern **Skövde** to the northeast, on the slopes of the Billingen mountain ridge, which is also home to some of Sweden's most creative computer game designers, as well as a key production site for Volvo.

VÄSTERGÖTLAND

🏠 Where to stay
1 Billingen recreation area tree tent *p74*
2 Bjertorp Slott *p74*
3 Hofsnäs Herrgård *p77*
4 Hotell Lassalyckan *p76*
5 Knistad Herrgård *p74*
6 Victoria House *p70*

✖ Where to eat and drink
7 Åsundsholm Golf & Country Club *p76*
   Bjertorp Slott (see 2)
8 Falbygdens Osteria *p73*
9 The Food Company *p75*
10 Glasets Hus café *p77*
11 Hellekis Trädgårdscafé *p71*
   Hofsnäs Herrgård (see 3)
   Hvita Hjorten (see 6)
   Knistad Herrgård (see 5)
12 Mattias Golfrestaurang *p74*
13 Mellbygatans *p70*
14 Nygrens Café *p78*
15 Sivans Ost *p73*

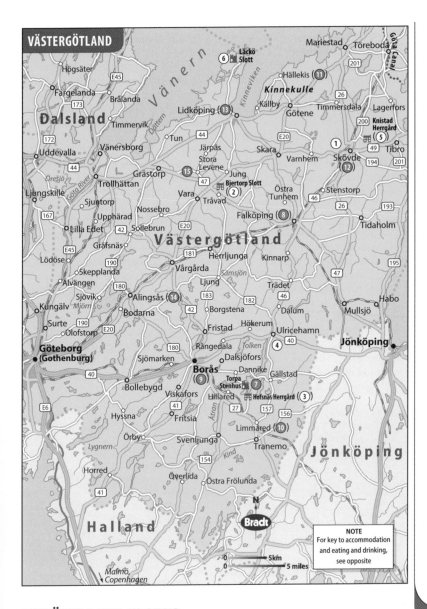

LIDKÖPING AND AROUND

Handsome **Lidköping** owes much of its good looks to an age-old decree stating that the height of a house may not exceed the width of the street on which it stands. This is particularly evident around the Lidan River in the centre of town where Lidköping's old town square, dating from 1446, stands elegantly facing the new town square, created by Magnus Gabriel de la Gardie (page 70) in 1671. Both squares still make for a pleasant wander, though the most appealing section of town to stroll around is Esplanaden where it runs across Mellbygatan overlooking the park, ablaze with flowers in summer.

The town's chief claim to fame, however, is the **Rörstrand Center** at Fabriksgatan 4 (**w** rorstrand-museum.se). Run by Europe's second-oldest porcelain firm (Rörstrand was founded in Stockholm in 1726), it's located by the lakeside just beyond the northern end of Norra Torngatan. Though the company is revered by many Swedes, the museum here is, perhaps, only of interest to visitors if you have a burning desire to see more plates than at a Greek wedding. A number of pleasing classical designs are on sale in the adjoining shop. For top-notch, locally sourced food, look no further than Mellbygatans (**w** mellbygatans.se) at Mellbygatan 10.

LÄCKÖ SLOTT (**w** lackoslott.se) Läckö Slott is everyone's idea of a fairy-tale castle:

its turrets and towers all creamy white and splendiferous. Overlooking Lake Vänern 25km north of Lidköping, today's Baroque castle actually began life as a military fortress in 1298, though its glory days didn't come until the late 17th century when it was owned by one of the leading personalities of the age: Count Magnus Gabriel de la Gardie (1622–86). De la Gardie introduced the Baroque ideal of symmetry and regularity to his home, adding a third floor in the process; the castle's exterior is the same today as it was in de la Gardie's day as it has been thoroughly restored. Inside, there's a wealth of exquisite decoration, particularly in the apartment which belonged to his German wife, Marie Eufrosyne. English-language guided tours run several times daily. Opposite the castle, Victoria House (**w** naturum.lackoslott.se; dbl rooms from 1,590kr) is a modern and comfortable hotel, which was creatively designed to blend in perfectly with the surrounding countryside. It also has an excellent restaurant, Hvita Hjorten, serving organic produce grown in the castle gardens, which are also worth a look whilst at Läckö. There's also a free nature centre (*naturum*) here with exhibitions about Lake Vänern and its wildlife; full details are available on the Victoria House website.

Baroque Läckö Slott overlooks Lake Vänern, Sweden's largest lake (Roger Borgelid)

Take a walk through Kinnekulle's charming meadows and woodland (Monika Mano)

KINNEKULLE The delightful upland region of Kinnekulle (pronounced roughly *shin-uh-kul-uh*), around 20km or so northeast of Lidköping, is one of the real treats of Västergötland. Although the area is very much of the mainland, it has a curiously insular feel to it and, indeed, the locals see themselves as living quite autonomously. Kinnekulle is dominated by a 300m high ridge at its centre which effectively separates it from the flatlands to the south and east, while to the north and west there is the vast expanse of Lake Vänern. The strange flat-topped shape of the hill is due to its top layer of hard volcanic rock which even 400 million years of Swedish weather has not managed to wear down, making for something of a botanical and geological treasure trove. For a great view of the plains to the south and the lake to the north, head up to the viewing tower (*utsiktstorn*) at **Högkullen**. At the northernmost point of Kinnekulle, the only town as such is **Hällekis**, a charming little place with a smattering of timber houses from the late 1800s though outside the centre several unlovely buildings remain from the town's heyday as a concrete manufacturer. However, the coastline to the west of the village is fabulous and you'll come across several little beaches where you can readily take a dip in the waters of Lake Vänern. Look out, too, for the **Munkängarna** meadows (just east of Råbäck train station) where the wild garlic (*ramslök* in Swedish), so prized as the key ingredient in the region's favourite soup, grows in abundance. Close by, just south of tiny Hällekis harbour, you'll find the idyllic Hellekis Trädgårdscafé (**w** hellekiscafe.se), where you can sample wild garlic soup (the house speciality), or their heavenly cake buffet, as you sit amid the vines in the orangery.

VARNHEM AND AROUND

Around 40km southeast of Lidköping, the village of Varnhem (14km west of Skövde) is today a leafy and peaceful little place tucked away in rural Västergötland. However, in medieval times Varnhem was an important religious centre – the Cistercian Order founded an **abbey** here in 1150 which operated for almost 400 years. Later, in the mid-17th century, the abbey **church** (**w** vastsverige.com/en/skara/produkter/varnhems-klosterkyrka; admission 40kr) was restored and today this remarkable stone structure, complete with its system of buttresses, is all that remains of the original abbey. Inside, you'll find the tomb of Swedish statesman Birger Jarl (1190–1266), who played a pivotal role in the consolidation of Sweden. In 2002 his grave was reopened for scientific analysis and it was confirmed that the bones inside were most likely those of the earl and his family.

KATA GÅRD (**w** vastsverige.com/en/skara/produkter/kata-gard) On the hill beside the abbey, archaeologists have discovered a vast **Viking-age graveyard**, containing some 3,000 graves and the well-preserved remains of a Christian church from the same period; Kata Gård is one of the most sensational finds ever made in Sweden since it provides proof that Varnhem was Christian an entire century before the rest of the country. A simple visitor centre, with a distinctive, steeply pitched, V-shaped roof, has now been constructed over the remains of the church's crypt, allowing visitors to walk over and view the walls from a raised walkway. However, it's the well-preserved **skeleton** of a woman in her 30s that really steals the show here: buried beside the church in the mid-1000s in a grave lined by solid limestone slabs and topped by a gravestone carved with a cross and runestones, the woman is thought to have owned the farm here. From the engraving, we know that 'Kättil made this stone for Kata, his wife, Torgil's sister' – the entire site has now been

The remarkable buttressed church is all that remains of the abbey at Varnhem (Jennie Lund)

FARM SHOPS

Agricultural Västergötland is awash with farm shops selling locally sourced organic produce. Two of the best are: **Sivans Ost** (w sivansost.se) at Oljeberget near Vara which stores – and sells – mature cheeses; there's a café and bakery here, too. Another fine cheese shop can be found in Falköping – **Falbygdens Osteria** (w falbygdensosteria.se) has more than 150 different cheeses from around the world.

A tempting selection of cheeses is available at Sivans Ost (Åsa Dahlgren)

named after Kata (*gård* is Swedish for 'farm'). **DNA analysis** has enabled scientists to ascertain that Kata had light brown hair and blueish-grey eyes – a life-size reconstruction has now been made and can be viewed in Västergötlands Museum (w vastergotlandsmuseum.se/kata-gard-varnhem) in nearby Skara along with an exhibition about the site and excavation work.

HORNBORGASJÖN (LAKE HORNBORGA) Roughly 5km south of Varnhem, Hornborgasjön is the scene of a remarkable natural spectacle every spring. Sometime between mid-March and the end of April, thousands of **cranes** (generally around 18,000 birds) arrive here from Spain to pair ahead of the mating season. They remain here for two or three weeks before continuing to northern Sweden for the summer. As part of their pairing ritual, the birds perform an elaborate dance around each other which attracts thousands of spectators every year. The 'crane dance', as it's known, is best viewed from the car parks at the southern end of the lake, off road 184 between Falköping and Skara, and there's a visitor centre and viewing tower on the eastern side of the lake. The birds return, albeit in smaller numbers, from the middle of August onwards as they begin their migration south for the winter. For more details see w visithornborgasjon.se. Skövde and Falköping are both gateways to the area with excellent links to Gothenburg.

EKORNAVALLEN (w vastsverige.com/falkoping; free entry) The ancient **burial site** of Ekornavallen, about 5km south of Hornborgasjön on the road between Broddetorp and Torbjörntorp, is quite simply breathtaking. Used over 4,000 years as a burial place for the dead, this vast site dating from the Stone Age consists of four walk-through passage **graves**, two **stone circles**, 12 **standing stones** and several **stone settings**. It is extremely unusual for a burial site to have been used over such a long period of time – allow yourself plenty of time to wander among the stone relics and appreciate this extraordinary place.

BJERTORP SLOTT (w bjertorpslott.se; dbl from 2,045kr) Around 30km directly south of Lidköping (or 45km southwest of Varnhem), Bjertorp Slott is a grand country manor house, completed in 1914, set in open countryside on the Västergötland plains. Designed by the same architect who was behind the iconic NK department store building in Stockholm, Fredrik Boberg, Bjertorp is every inch the country residence of one of Sweden's leading industrialists of the day, Knut Henrik Littorin, who made his fortune working for Alfred Nobel's oil business in Russia. The manor house is built of limestone atop foundations of granite, while inside there are oak panels, ornate staircases and grandiose chandeliers seemingly everywhere you look. The **restaurant** here is, as you would expect, top-notch.

SKÖVDE AND AROUND

The main town in these parts is Skövde (roughly pronounced *shuv-duh*), a no-nonsense, workaday sort of a place, that is never going to win any beauty contests. Home to one of **Volvo's** key production sites (car and truck engines are made here) and an ever-expanding centre for **computer game design** and creation (the renowned Goat Simulator was born here), Skövde's main downtown attraction is **Arena Skövde** (w arenaskovde.se), an impressive water park, replete with adventure slides and an impressive sauna complex. As un-culinary as it may sound, a tasty stop for lunch is the town's golf course, where the winning **restaurant** (w mattiasmat.se) is overseen by leading chef, Mattias Hägg, who certainly knows his apron from his shrimp.

BILLINGEN RECREATION AREA (w billingen.nu) A visit to the Billingen recreation area, just outside town at Arne Sandbergs väg, really thrills. Billingen is a classic, rectangular-shaped, flat-topped table mountain, reaching 300m in height, which is ideal for skiing, snowshoe walking, cycling, running and hiking. There's also a 50m open-air **swimming pool** up here, Billingebadet, from where the views over the surrounding plains and forestland are quite something. A unique way to get close to nature up on the ridgetop is to spend a night in a **tree-tent**, an ingenious trampoline-like contraption with a tent on it, suspended off the ground by three sturdy straps, tied to nearby trees; book via Älska Billingen (↳ 0736/13 44 01; ⓕ alskabillingen).

KNISTAD HERRGÅRD (w knistad.se) Barely 10km northeast of Skövde, Knistad Herrgård is an elegant country manor house that specialises in golfing. Having worked your way round the adjoining golf course during the day, you can enjoy some well-prepared food in the manor house's own restaurant in the evening. Accommodation is located in the 'wings' to the main building which, sadly, lack the ornate flourishes of the manor house itself.

BORÅS AND AROUND

While Borås may not be top of the itinerary on your trip to West Sweden, this industrial town, around 60km east of Gothenburg, is trying hard to reinvent itself. Over the years, Borås predominantly made a name for itself in the production of textiles: you name it, seemingly everything from men's socks to women's bras has been made here. Today, it is this rich industrial heritage which the town is keen to show off: the **Textilmuséet** (w textilmuseet.se), inside the Textile Fashion Center at Skaraborgsvägen 3A, does a valiant job at bringing the past to life through a range of well-conceived exhibitions – check out, in particular, the long line of machines imported from the UK and Germany for the production of cotton, as well as the glorious jumble of Singer sewing machines. There's a decent café and restaurant here, too, **The Food Company** (w thecompany.se), which serves a range of organic produce.

The road from women's corsets to art is, admittedly, not an immediately obvious one. Yet, that is exactly what one of the big hitters in Borås has done: Abecita Corsettindustri did indeed begin life making the likes of 18-hour girdles but has now cast off its association with women's knickers in favour of exhibiting a changing collection of photography and pop art. **Abecita Konstmuseum** (w abecitakonst.se), Herrljungagatan 15, holds work by David Hockney, Andy Warhol and Francis Bacon among its treasures and is well worth a visit.

During your exploration of Borås, you can't fail to notice the vast amount of murals and other art works which adorn the city centre. The murals are all part of what Borås calls **No Limit Street Art** (w nolimitboras.com), an orgy of urban street painting which takes place in the city every few years. The biannual event draws artists from several different countries who are presented with entire walls of buildings and random urban spaces to daub with graffiti and other expressions of their art. There are more details at w vastsverige.com/en/Cultural_experiences/Boras-world-leader-in-innovative-design-and-street-art.

The murals that adorn the walls and buildings of Borås are part of No Limit Street Art, a festival of urban street painting that takes place every few years (Jonas Ingman)

ULRICEHAMN Heading east from Borås, it's a straightforward drive of around 40km to likeable Ulricehamn, a shy-and-retiring little place, which clambers up the hillside above the eastern shores of Lake Åsunden. Arguably, the main attraction in town is the elegant Kallbadhus, the cold-water bathing house, which sits atop a wooden jetty, reaching gingerly out into the shallow waters of Åsunden. Indeed, Ulricehamn began life as a genteel health resort during the late 1800s, profiting from its lakeside location. Today, though, the town is better known as the location of one of Scandinavia's most popular artificial snow facilities, Lassalyckan, with its extensive 30km network of cross-country ski tracks and comfortable, country hotel (**w** hotell-lassalyckan.se; dbl from 1,225kr). The town also boasts a modest downhill facility, the Ulricehamn Ski Center (**w** uc-skidcenter.se) with a ski school for beginners. During summer, there's mountain biking, orienteering and hiking to choose from. For a bite to eat, look no further than **Åsundsholm Golf & Country Club** (**w** asundsholm. se), just 20 minutes away, near the southern end of Lake Åsunden, in nearby Vegby. The restaurant here prides itself on serving locally sourced produce.

In winter, cross-country skiing is a popular activity in Ulricehamn (Roger Borgelid)

Torpa Stenhus is a perfectly preserved medieval castle (Jonas Ingman)

TORPA STENHUS (**w** torpastenhus.se) Around 30km south of Ulricehamn lies one of West Sweden's finest sights: Torpa Stenhus, a perfectly preserved medieval castle dating, in parts, from around 1470, beautifully located on the shores of Lake Åsunden. As the Swedish name suggests, the castle was built of stone as a means of protection from Danish troops – at the time much of what is now southern Sweden was part of Denmark. During the 16th century the building was reconstructed and an extension was added around 1550 ahead of a visit by King Gustav Vasa. Indeed, the original table that the king sat at and a wall painting in ash from 1590 are two of the most remarkable exhibits inside the castle. Superbly executed guided tours of the castle are available in English and are a fantastic way of learning about the history of this remarkably well-preserved medieval castle. Just 4km away, on the eastern shore of Åsunden, you'll find **Hofsnäs Herrgård** (**w** hofsnas.se), an idyllically located old manor house with a great restaurant and limited accommodation.

LIMMARED An easy drive of around 18km from Hofsnäs Herrgård will bring you to the little village of Limmared, which is also connected to Gothenburg by train. Indeed, right next to the train station on Östra Järnvägsgatan, you'll find the town's former glassworks, transformed today into **Glasets Hus** (**w** glasetshuslimmared.se), an engaging mix of museum, café and glassblowing workshop. Having cantered through the exhibition of glassware where seemingly everything from chandeliers to medicine bottles is available for perusal, it's time to turn your hand to the exciting business of glassblowing. With the help of the experts, you'll be able to turn and blow your own glass vase or bottle and even have it sent home to you after it's been through the hardening process in the kiln. Before you leave, have a look at the items produced by Glas af Limmered which are handmade on site and available for purchase.

ALINGSÅS (w kafestaden.se) If there's one thing that defines Alingsås, a pretty little place 40km northwest of Borås on the banks of the Lillån River, it's coffee. Indeed, the town has been big on cafés since the 1700s when the industrial revolution drew women out of the home and into the workplace. Quite why this movement produced so many cafés in precisely Alingsås (the industrial development occurred right across Sweden, of course), locals are at a loss to explain. Be that as it may, seemingly hapless husbands were unable to cook for themselves and began frequenting cafés for their meals – and a cup of coffee. Today, one of the most pleasurable things to do in Alingsås is to take a guided tour of some of the town's cafés and partake of that most hallowed tradition in Sweden,

Princess cake is a Swedish classic (Jonas Ingman)

the *fika* – a cup of coffee and a bun. There's a whole variety of different cafés dotted across town and every local has their own favourite – one of the most popular is the venerable Nygrens Café (w nygrenscafe.se) at Drottninggatan 27, complete with ornate wallpaper and elegant old furniture.

WEST SWEDEN ONLINE

For additional online content, articles, photos and more on West Sweden, why not visit w bradtguides.com/westsweden?

FOLLOW US

Tag us in your posts to share your adventures using this guide with us – we'd love to hear from you.

- **f** BradtTravelGuides & West Sweden including Gothenburg
- **🐦** @BradtGuides & @WestSwedenTB
- **📷** @bradtguides & @westsweden
- **P** bradtguides
- **▶** bradtguides & VastsverigeTV

Appendix

GETTING STARTED IN SWEDISH

English	Swedish	Pronunciation
Hello	Hej	*hay*
How are you?	Hur mår du?	*hoor more doo?*
Fine, thanks	Bara bra, tack	*baa-ra braa, tak*
That's great	Det är jättebra	*day err yet-uh braa*
Thanks a lot	Tack så mycket	*tak so muck-uh*
Excuse me	Ursäkta	*oor-sheck-ta*
Please	Vänligen	*van-lee-uhn*
I come from…	Jag kommer från…	*yaa komm-uh fron…*
Are you from Gothenburg?	Kommer du från Göteborg?	*komm-uh doo fron yur-ter-bori?*
Can I have?	Kan jag få?	*kan yaa fo?*
Do you have…?	Har du…?	*haar doo…?*
A coffee with milk	En kaffe med mjölk	*ayn kaff-eh me myulk*
A large beer, please	En stor stark, tack	*ayn stoor shtark, tak*
How much is that?	Hur mycket kostar det?	*hoor muck-uk kost-ah day?*
Bye	Hejdå	*hay doh*

KEY TO SYMBOLS

— — —	International border	🛈	Tourist information
· · · · ·	Provincial border	✉	Post office
· · · · · · · ·	Göta Canal	🏛	Historic/important building
▬▬▬	Motorway	🏰	Castle/fortress
▬▬▬	Main road	⁘	Historic site
———	Other road	☻	Museum/gallery
┅┅┅	Railway	🎭	Theatre/cinema
··········	Pedestrian street	†	Church
→	One way street	🪦	Cemetery
✈	Airport	✿	Garden
🚌	Bus station	●	Other point of interest
–⛴–	Vehicle ferry	▲	Summit (height in metres)
–⛴–	Passenger ferry	🤸	Sporting venue
🅿	Parking		Urban park
⛽	Petrol station		National park/reserve

Note: Bracketed listings shown straight after the name of a town or village are situated within that location. Gothenburg maps use grid lines to allow easy location of sites, which are given in square brackets with page number followed by grid number, eg: [14 C1].

Index

Page numbers in **bold** indicate major entries; those in *italics* indicate maps